# PERSONAL DEVELOPMENT FOR INTROVERTED ENTREPRENEURS

Shah Rukh

# CONTENTS

# INTRODUCTION

In a world that often celebrates the extroverted and outspoken, there exists a quiet yet potent force of entrepreneurs who thrive in their unique introspective nature – the introverted entrepreneurs. This book, "Personal Development for Introverted Entrepreneurs," celebrates and empowers those who possess the power of deep thought, creativity, and unwavering determination within the entrepreneurial landscape.

For far too long, introverted individuals may have felt overshadowed or underestimated in the fast-paced world of business. Yet, contrary to misconceptions, their introverted traits are not limitations but powerful assets that can lead to groundbreaking innovation, empathetic leadership, and sustainable success. By understanding, nurturing, and embracing these innate strengths, introverted entrepreneurs can carve a path to achievement that aligns with their true selves and brings them fulfillment like no other.

The journey of an introverted entrepreneur is a unique one, characterized by the quiet resilience that propels them forward through challenges and setbacks. In this book, we delve into the art of personal development specifically tailored to the introverted entrepreneurial spirit. From harnessing introverted leadership to mastering the art of networking, from embracing self-awareness to fostering a growth mindset, we explore a holistic approach to personal growth and achievement that empowers introverted entrepreneurs to flourish on their terms.

Throughout these chapters, we seek to foster an environment that celebrates the inherent qualities of introverted entrepreneurship.

We aim to inspire introverted individuals to embrace their authentic selves, unapologetically, and break free from the constraints of societal expectations. This book is a guide to unlocking the true potential within introverted entrepreneurs, where they can confidently navigate the ever-evolving business landscape while staying true to their principles and values.

Drawing upon the power of introspection, this book will explore the unique traits that introverted entrepreneurs possess, such as the art of active listening, the ability to cultivate meaningful connections, and the strength to overcome adversity with quiet resilience. By honing these qualities, introverted entrepreneurs can create businesses that not only succeed but make a profound impact in their industries and the lives of their stakeholders.

As we embark on this journey of personal development for introverted entrepreneurs, we invite you to discover the power within yourself – the power to embrace your introverted nature and thrive in your own authentic way. This book serves as a beacon of support and guidance, offering insights, strategies, and stories of success that will empower you to celebrate your unique strengths and embark on a fulfilling and purpose-driven entrepreneurial journey.

Welcome to "Personal Development for Introverted Entrepreneurs." Let us embark on this transformative quest together, embracing our true selves, and unlocking the boundless potential that lies within each one of us.

# CHAPTER 1: EMBRACING YOUR INTROVERSION: A STRENGTH FOR ENTREPRENEURSHIP

Introduction:

In a world that often celebrates extroversion and outgoing personalities, it is essential to recognize and embrace the unique qualities that introverts bring to the table, especially in the realm of entrepreneurship. This chapter delves into the empowering journey of embracing one's introversion and understanding how it can be a distinctive asset for aspiring and established entrepreneurs alike.

1.  Defining Introversion:

Introversion is a personality trait characterized by a preference for internal reflection, solitary activities, and a need for downtime to recharge after social interactions. Unlike extroverts who thrive in social settings, introverts tend to draw energy from within and may find large groups or constant external stimulation draining. Understanding the core characteristics of introversion is the first step in recognizing its potential as a strength in entrepreneurship.

2.  The Power of Self-Awareness:

Embracing one's introversion starts with developing a deep sense of self-awareness. Entrepreneurs who recognize their introverted tendencies can better understand their energy levels, preferred work environments, and communication styles. This awareness enables them to make informed decisions, build effective strategies, and establish boundaries that align with their authentic selves.

3.  The Introvert's Unique Perspective:

Introverted entrepreneurs possess a unique lens through which they view the world. Their introspective nature allows them to observe details, notice patterns, and make thoughtful decisions. This distinct perspective can lead to innovative solutions, creative problem-solving, and a deeper understanding of their target audience's needs.

### 4. Embracing Introverted Leadership:

Contrary to the stereotype of the charismatic extroverted leader, introverts have a leadership style that emphasizes listening, thoughtful decision-making, and fostering a collaborative and inclusive environment. Introverted entrepreneurs often excel at creating a supportive team culture where every member's input is valued, leading to increased employee satisfaction and loyalty.

### 5. The Strength of One-on-One Connections:

Introverts tend to excel in one-on-one interactions due to their ability to actively listen and empathize. In the entrepreneurial world, building strong and meaningful connections with clients, partners, and team members is crucial for success. Introverted entrepreneurs can leverage their natural inclination for deeper connections to nurture long-lasting relationships.

### 6. The Art of Introverted Networking:

Traditional networking events may be overwhelming for introverts, but they possess the skills to network effectively in their own way. By focusing on smaller gatherings, attending industry-specific events, or participating in online communities, introverted entrepreneurs can form authentic connections and build a solid network of like-minded individuals.

### 7. Embracing Introversion in Marketing:

Introverted entrepreneurs can craft powerful marketing strategies that align with their personalities. Content marketing, thought leadership, and storytelling are just some of the marketing techniques that allow introverts to shine without feeling the pressure of aggressive self-promotion.

### 8. Embracing Introversion in Sales:

The idea of being a salesperson might seem daunting to many introverts, but they can excel in sales by leveraging their listening skills and understanding the needs of potential clients. By focusing on providing value and building trust, introverted entrepreneurs can create genuine connections that lead to long-term customer relationships.

9. Leveraging Introversion in Problem-Solving:

Introverts' penchant for contemplation and deep analysis can be a powerful tool when it comes to problem-solving. Their ability to think critically and consider multiple perspectives can lead to innovative solutions that may not have been apparent to others.

10. Creating an Introvert-Friendly Work Environment:

Entrepreneurs who embrace their introversion can foster a work environment that supports introverted strengths and encourages open communication. This might involve offering flexible work hours, quiet spaces for focused work, and encouraging written communication in addition to verbal.

Conclusion:

Embracing introversion as a strength for entrepreneurship requires self-awareness, confidence, and a willingness to challenge societal expectations. By recognizing the unique qualities that introverts possess, entrepreneurs can harness their inherent strengths to drive innovation, build meaningful connections, and create successful businesses that reflect their authentic selves. Embracing introversion is not about trying to change one's personality but rather celebrating it as a valuable asset in the entrepreneurial journey.

# CHAPTER 2: UNDERSTANDING INTROVERSION: UNRAVELLING YOUR UNIQUE TRAITS

Introduction:

To fully embrace introversion as a strength in entrepreneurship, it is essential to gain a deep understanding of what introversion truly means. This chapter aims to delve into the intricacies of introversion, exploring the psychological, behavioural, and physiological aspects that shape the unique traits of introverted individuals. By unravelling these traits, aspiring and established introverted entrepreneurs can harness their distinct advantages and navigate their entrepreneurial journey with greater self-awareness and confidence.

1. The Psychology of Introversion:

At its core, introversion is a personality trait that is relatively stable throughout an individual's life. Psychologists like Carl Jung first introduced the concept, emphasizing that introverts tend to direct their energy inward, focusing on their inner thoughts and emotions rather than external stimuli. Understanding this psychological foundation lays the groundwork for recognizing introversion's influence on an entrepreneur's behaviours and decision-making processes.

2. Introverted Behaviour:

Introverted behaviour is characterized by a preference for solitude or intimate social interactions over large gatherings. Introverts often find meaningful connections with a select group of close friends and may value quality over quantity when it comes to social interactions. They may also enjoy activities that provide ample time for introspection, such as reading, writing, or engaging in creative pursuits.

3. Introverted Energy Management:

An essential aspect of understanding introversion is the concept of energy management. Introverts tend to feel more energized and rejuvenated after spending time alone or engaging in solitary activities. They may find social interactions draining, especially in noisy or crowded environments. As such, introverted entrepreneurs must be mindful of managing their energy levels to maintain productivity and overall well-being.

4. Sensitivity to Stimuli:

Introverts often exhibit heightened sensitivity to external stimuli, such as bright lights, loud noises, or bustling environments. This sensitivity can influence their preferences for calm and peaceful surroundings, allowing them to focus more effectively on tasks and make thoughtful decisions without distractions.

5. Deep Thinkers and Reflective Nature:

Introverts are known for their contemplative nature and tendency to think deeply about various topics. They may spend considerable time reflecting on their experiences and ideas, which can lead to insights, creativity, and strategic planning in the entrepreneurial realm.

6. Emotional Depth and Empathy:

Introverted individuals often display emotional depth and a strong capacity for empathy. They can connect with others on a profound level, making them effective leaders and communicators when it comes to understanding and addressing the needs of team members, clients, and customers.

7. Communication Styles:

Introverts may prefer written communication or one-on-one conversations, where they can fully engage and express their thoughts without interruption. They may find public speaking or group presentations challenging, but this preference does not diminish their ability to articulate ideas effectively.

### 8. Introverted Processing:

Introverts tend to process information internally before sharing it externally. This inward processing allows them to consider various perspectives and weigh the pros and cons before communicating their conclusions. This trait can be advantageous in decision-making and problem-solving scenarios.

### 9. Neurological Differences:

Neurological studies have revealed that introverts' brains may have different patterns of activation compared to extroverts. These differences can influence how introverts respond to stimuli, process information, and experience the world around them.

### 10. Nature vs. Nurture:

While introversion is considered an inherent trait, its expression can be influenced by both nature and nurture. Environmental factors, life experiences, and cultural norms may shape how introverted tendencies are manifested in different individuals.

Conclusion:

Understanding introversion goes beyond recognizing surface-level stereotypes. By unravelling the unique traits of introverted individuals, entrepreneurs can gain valuable insights into their own strengths, preferences, and challenges. Armed with this knowledge, introverted entrepreneurs can navigate their entrepreneurial journey with authenticity, self-acceptance, and a clearer sense of how their introverted traits can be harnessed to thrive in the dynamic world of business. Embracing and leveraging these unique traits can empower introverted entrepreneurs to contribute their distinctive perspectives, innovate with empathy, and create businesses that align with their true selves.

# CHAPTER 3: HARNESSING INTROVERTED LEADERSHIP: QUIET POWER IN BUSINESS

Introduction:

In a world that often associates leadership with charisma and extroversion, introverted individuals possess a unique and powerful leadership style. This chapter delves into the concept of harnessing introverted leadership, showcasing how the qualities inherent to introverts can create a positive impact on businesses. We will explore the various aspects of quiet power and how it can be effectively leveraged to lead teams, drive innovation, and foster a culture of collaboration and growth.

1. Redefining Leadership:

Introverted leadership challenges the traditional view of leadership as being loud and assertive. Instead, it emphasizes the value of deep listening, thoughtfulness, and leading by example. By redefining leadership in this manner, introverted entrepreneurs can unlock their potential as influential and inspiring leaders.

2. The Strength of Quiet Confidence:

Introverted leaders exude quiet confidence that emanates from their self-assuredness and expertise. Their ability to reflect before acting enables them to make well-considered decisions, fostering a sense of trust and stability among their teams.

3. Empowering Team Members:

Introverted leaders excel in empowering team members to contribute their best work. By actively listening to their team's ideas and encouraging open communication, they create an inclusive and collaborative environment where everyone feels valued and supported.

4. Leading by Example:

Introverted leaders demonstrate the behaviours they expect from their team members. Through their commitment to hard work, dedication, and ethical practices, they inspire their teams to follow suit, cultivating a culture of integrity and excellence.

5. Effective Communication:

While introverts may not be naturally inclined to dominate conversations, their thoughtful communication style ensures that their messages carry weight and impact. They carefully choose their words, making every interaction meaningful and purposeful.

6. Creating Space for Diverse Perspectives:

Introverted leaders understand the value of diverse perspectives and actively encourage their team members to share their ideas. By creating an environment that welcomes different viewpoints, they unlock the potential for innovation and creative problem-solving.

7. Resolving Conflict with Diplomacy:

Conflict is an inevitable part of any business environment. Introverted leaders approach conflict resolution with diplomacy, seeking win-win solutions and striving to maintain harmonious relationships among team members.

8. Leading in Times of Change:

During times of change and uncertainty, introverted leaders offer stability and reassurance. Their composed demeanour helps ease anxiety and encourages their teams to adapt and embrace new challenges with resilience.

9. Balancing Introversion and Extroversion:

While introverted leaders excel in many areas, they also recognize the importance of leveraging the strengths of their extroverted team members. By finding a balance between introversion and extroversion, they create a well-rounded and high-performing team.

### 10. Nurturing Introverted Leadership in Others:

Introverted leaders also have a unique opportunity to nurture and mentor emerging introverted leaders within their organizations. By recognizing and developing leadership potential in others, they contribute to a future generation of effective and empathetic leaders.

### 11. Inspiring Trust and Loyalty:

The calm and thoughtful approach of introverted leaders fosters a sense of trust and loyalty among their team members. This foundation of trust is essential for building long-lasting relationships and a strong organizational culture.

### 12. Leading in Introvert-Friendly Environments:

Introverted leaders can create workspaces that cater to the needs of introverted team members. This might involve providing quiet areas for focused work, flexible working hours, or digital communication channels that allow for thoughtful responses.

Conclusion:

Harnessing introverted leadership in business is about embracing the power of quiet influence, deep connections, and thoughtful decision-making. Introverted leaders have the capacity to create a positive and meaningful impact on their teams, businesses, and the wider community. By understanding and celebrating the unique strengths of introversion, entrepreneurs can cultivate a new paradigm of leadership that emphasizes empathy, collaboration, and sustained success. Embracing introverted leadership enables businesses to thrive, drawing upon the quiet power that lies within their introverted leaders to shape a more compassionate and innovative future.

# CHAPTER 4: CULTIVATING SELF-AWARENESS: THE FOUNDATION OF PERSONAL GROWTH

Introduction:

In the journey of personal and professional development, self-awareness serves as the cornerstone upon which all other growth is built. This chapter delves into the significance of cultivating self-awareness and how it acts as a guiding force for entrepreneurs in their pursuit of success and fulfillment. Understanding oneself at a deep level allows entrepreneurs to make informed decisions, navigate challenges with resilience, and create a purpose-driven path towards personal and business growth.

1.  The Essence of Self-Awareness:

Self-awareness is the ability to objectively recognize and understand one's emotions, thoughts, strengths, weaknesses, and behaviours. It involves introspection, reflection, and a willingness to confront both positive and negative aspects of oneself. Entrepreneurs who cultivate self-awareness embark on a transformative journey of growth and authenticity.

2.  Unearthing Core Values and Beliefs:

To build a strong foundation of self-awareness, entrepreneurs must explore their core values and beliefs. Understanding what truly matters to them allows for better decision-making aligned with their principles, which ultimately contributes to building a purpose-driven and meaningful business.

3.  Embracing Strengths and Weaknesses:

Self-aware entrepreneurs acknowledge their strengths and leverage them to excel in their areas of expertise. Additionally, they accept their weaknesses as opportunities for growth and seek ways to address them through learning, skill development, or team collaboration.

4. Recognizing Emotional Intelligence:

Self-awareness goes hand-in-hand with emotional intelligence. Entrepreneurs who are in tune with their emotions can better manage stress, navigate interpersonal relationships, and communicate effectively with team members, clients, and partners.

5. Understanding Triggers and Reactions:

By recognizing personal triggers and understanding reactive patterns, entrepreneurs gain the ability to respond thoughtfully rather than impulsively. This level of self-awareness fosters healthier interactions and decision-making in high-pressure situations.

6. The Impact of Past Experiences:

Exploring past experiences and their impact on one's present mindset and behaviours is essential for growth. Entrepreneurs can identify patterns, heal from past traumas, and use these insights to shape a more empowering future.

7. Embracing Feedback and Criticism:

Self-aware entrepreneurs are open to feedback and criticism, valuing these insights as opportunities for improvement. Constructive feedback becomes a catalyst for growth, allowing them to refine their skills and approach.

8. Navigating Limiting Beliefs:

Self-awareness helps entrepreneurs identify and challenge limiting beliefs that might hinder their progress. By replacing negative thought patterns with positive affirmations, they create a mindset that fosters resilience and perseverance.

9. Developing Empathy and Understanding Others:

Understanding oneself paves the way for understanding others on a deeper level. Empathy, a crucial skill for effective leadership and collaboration, stems from recognizing and empathizing with one's own emotions and experiences.

10. The Role of Mindfulness and Reflection:

Mindfulness practices, such as meditation and journaling, foster self-awareness by encouraging introspection and reflection. Entrepreneurs who make time for such practices gain clarity, reduce stress, and make better decisions.

11. Embracing Vulnerability:

Self-awareness requires vulnerability – the willingness to be honest and open about one's thoughts, feelings, and aspirations. Embracing vulnerability creates authentic connections and fosters trust within teams and business relationships.

12. Setting Authentic Goals:

Entrepreneurs who cultivate self-awareness set authentic and meaningful goals that align with their true desires. This process ensures that their entrepreneurial journey is purpose-driven, fulfilling, and aligned with their personal values.

Conclusion:

Cultivating self-awareness is a lifelong journey that fuels personal growth and professional success. As the foundation of all development, self-awareness enables entrepreneurs to navigate their challenges, build authentic connections, and lead with empathy and resilience. Embracing self-awareness empowers entrepreneurs to create a life and business that is aligned with their true selves, resulting in greater fulfillment, meaningful contributions to society, and a legacy that leaves a positive impact on future generations. Through introspection, mindfulness, and a commitment to continuous growth, entrepreneurs can harness the power of self-awareness to embark on a transformative journey that leads to both personal and business success.

# CHAPTER 5: LEVERAGING INTROVERTED NETWORKING: BUILDING MEANINGFUL CONNECTIONS

Introduction:

Networking is an essential aspect of entrepreneurship, but it can be intimidating, particularly for introverted individuals who prefer more intimate and meaningful connections. In this chapter, we explore how introverted entrepreneurs can leverage their unique strengths to build authentic and impactful networks. By understanding the power of introverted networking, entrepreneurs can cultivate genuine relationships, foster collaboration, and create a supportive community that fuels their business growth.

1. Rethinking Networking for Introverts:

Introverted networking is not about attending every large-scale event or exchanging business cards with countless strangers. Instead, it involves a purposeful and strategic approach that emphasizes quality over quantity.

2. Embracing Meaningful Connections:

Introverted entrepreneurs excel at forming deep and meaningful connections. They focus on building a smaller network of like-minded individuals with whom they share genuine interests and values, fostering an environment of mutual support and respect.

3. The Power of Active Listening:

Introverted networking thrives on the power of active listening. By genuinely engaging in conversations and showing interest in others' perspectives, introverted entrepreneurs create a rapport that forms the foundation of lasting connections.

4. Nurturing Relationships Over Time:

Introverts prefer nurturing existing relationships rather than constantly seeking new ones. They invest time and effort in understanding and supporting their network, leading to trust and loyalty within the community.

5. Leveraging Digital Platforms:

Digital networking platforms can be a valuable tool for introverted entrepreneurs. Engaging in online communities, forums, and social media allows them to connect with like-minded individuals while leveraging their strengths in written communication.

6. Intentional Networking Events:

Rather than attending every networking event, introverted entrepreneurs can be selective and intentional about the gatherings they choose to participate in. Targeted events that align with their interests and goals enable them to make more meaningful connections.

7. The Art of Follow-Up:

Introverted networking extends beyond the initial interaction. Effective follow-up and maintaining connections over time are key to solidifying relationships and demonstrating genuine interest in others' endeavours.

8. Creating Introvert-Friendly Spaces:

As introverted entrepreneurs host networking events or gatherings, they can create environments that cater to the preferences of introverts. This might include providing quiet corners for conversation, facilitating small group discussions, or encouraging one-on-one interactions.

9. Collaborative Projects:

Introverted networking can lead to valuable collaborations with individuals who share complementary skills and goals. By joining forces with like-minded partners, introverted entrepreneurs can achieve more significant outcomes in their ventures.

### 10. Building an Introvert-Friendly Team:

When assembling a team, introverted entrepreneurs can recognize the value of both introverted and extroverted team members. An inclusive team culture that appreciates diverse communication styles and work preferences fosters a positive and productive environment.

### 11. Empowering Intentional Networking:

Introverted entrepreneurs can empower their network members to support and refer each other. By nurturing a community that values collaboration and mutual growth, they create a robust network that benefits everyone involved.

### 12. Overcoming Networking Challenges:

Networking can be challenging for introverts, but by recognizing their strengths and setting realistic expectations, they can gradually expand their comfort zone and develop effective networking skills.

Conclusion:

Introverted networking is not about conforming to traditional extroverted networking norms. Instead, it is an approach that leverages the unique strengths of introverted individuals to build meaningful and enduring connections. By embracing active listening, nurturing relationships, and creating intentional networking opportunities, introverted entrepreneurs can cultivate an authentic and supportive network that contributes to their personal and business growth. In the realm of introverted networking, quality outweighs quantity, and the impact of genuine connections resonates far beyond the boundaries of professional encounters. As introverted entrepreneurs harness the power of their networking style, they create a community of individuals who share values, aspirations, and a collective commitment to mutual success.

# CHAPTER 6: NAVIGATING EXTROVERTED ENVIRONMENTS: THRIVING AS AN INTROVERT

Introduction:

In a world that often celebrates extroversion and rewards loud, gregarious behaviour, introverts may find themselves in environments that feel overwhelming and challenging. This chapter explores the art of navigating extroverted environments as an introvert. By understanding their unique strengths and adopting strategies to preserve energy and thrive, introverts can embrace these settings while staying true to themselves and excelling in various situations.

1.  Recognizing the Value of Introversion:

Before venturing into extroverted environments, introverts should recognize and embrace the value they bring to the table. Introverted traits, such as deep thinking, active listening, and empathy, offer distinct advantages in collaborative settings.

2.  Setting Clear Boundaries:

In extroverted environments, it is crucial for introverts to set clear boundaries to protect their energy levels. Knowing when to take breaks, setting time limits for social interactions, and communicating personal needs are essential for maintaining well-being.

3.  The Power of Preparation:

Introverts often shine when they are well-prepared for social engagements. Taking time to research topics, anticipate questions, and gather information beforehand boosts confidence and facilitates meaningful interactions.

4.  Finding Supportive Allies:

Seeking out like-minded individuals or supportive allies in extroverted environments can create a sense of belonging. Forming genuine connections with these individuals offers a safety net and encourages introverts to engage more comfortably.

5.  Leveraging Active Listening:

Active listening is a superpower for introverts. In extroverted environments, introverts can use this skill to their advantage by truly understanding others, fostering deeper connections, and contributing thoughtfully to discussions.

6.  Embracing Selective Socializing:

Introverts may feel pressured to engage in every social activity in extroverted settings, but they should embrace selective socializing. Choosing meaningful events and interactions allows for more genuine connections.

7.  Recognizing Restorative Solitude:

After navigating extroverted environments, introverts require restorative solitude to recharge their energy. Taking time for introspection and self-care enables them to maintain balance and resilience.

8.  The Role of Body Language:

Introverts can use body language to communicate their engagement and interest in extroverted environments. Open postures, maintaining eye contact, and active listening cues show others that they are fully present.

9.  Embracing the Power of Yes and No:

Saying "yes" to opportunities that align with personal values and goals while being unafraid to say "no" to overwhelming or irrelevant demands empowers introverts to navigate extroverted environments with intention.

10. Engaging in Small Groups:

Introverts often thrive in smaller group settings. By seeking out or creating smaller gatherings within extroverted environments, they can foster deeper connections and feel more at ease.

### 11. Building Inner Confidence:

Cultivating inner confidence helps introverts navigate extroverted environments with self-assurance. Recognizing their unique strengths and contributions builds the foundation for thriving in any social setting.

### 12. Celebrating Authenticity:

Thriving as an introvert in extroverted environments is about celebrating authenticity. Embracing one's introverted nature and owning it with pride fosters respect and admiration from others.

Conclusion:

While extroverted environments may present challenges for introverts, they can navigate these settings with confidence and authenticity. By recognizing the value, they bring, setting boundaries, preparing effectively, and embracing their unique strengths, introverts can excel in any social situation. Navigating extroverted environments is not about changing who they are but rather leveraging their innate abilities to foster meaningful connections, contribute thoughtfully, and make a lasting impact. As introverts embrace the art of thriving in extroverted environments, they will find that their authenticity, empathy, and deep understanding of others become invaluable assets, driving personal growth and professional success in any setting they encounter.

# CHAPTER 7: THE ART OF EFFECTIVE COMMUNICATION: SPEAKING WITH IMPACT

Introduction:

Effective communication is an indispensable skill for success in both personal and professional realms. In this chapter, we delve into the art of mastering communication to deliver messages with impact. From public speaking to interpersonal interactions, introverted entrepreneurs can harness their unique strengths to engage and influence their audience, foster meaningful connections, and drive positive outcomes.

1. Understanding the Power of Communication:

Communication is the lifeblood of human interaction. It involves not only verbal expression but also non-verbal cues, active listening, and empathy. Recognizing the influence of communication in various aspects of life motivates introverted entrepreneurs to enhance their communication skills.

2. The Strengths of Introverted Communication:

Introverted entrepreneurs have innate strengths that shape their communication style. Active listening, thoughtful responses, and empathy enable them to create authentic connections and contribute meaningfully to conversations.

3. Preparing for Effective Communication:

Preparation is key to effective communication. Introverted entrepreneurs can capitalize on their inclination for detail-oriented planning to structure their messages, anticipate potential questions, and organize their thoughts cohesively.

4. Building Confidence:

Confidence plays a vital role in effective communication. Introverted entrepreneurs can build self-assurance through practice, focusing on their expertise, and recognizing their unique value in sharing insights and ideas.

### 5. Public Speaking for Introverts:

Public speaking is a common fear among introverts, but it is a skill that can be mastered. Techniques such as visualization, controlled breathing, and connecting with the audience help introverted entrepreneurs deliver impactful presentations.

### 6. Emphasizing Storytelling:

Storytelling is a powerful tool for engaging and captivating audiences. Introverted entrepreneurs can leverage their reflective nature to craft compelling narratives that resonate with their listeners.

### 7. Listening with Empathy:

Empathetic listening is a hallmark of introverted communication. By genuinely understanding others' perspectives, introverted entrepreneurs create a foundation of trust and respect in their interactions.

### 8. Balancing Verbal and Non-Verbal Communication:

Introverted entrepreneurs should be mindful of their non-verbal cues, as body language plays a significant role in communication. Maintaining eye contact, open postures, and expressive gestures enhance the impact of their words.

### 9. Adapting Communication Styles:

Effective communication involves adapting to different audiences and situations. Introverted entrepreneurs can tailor their communication style to suit the preferences and needs of their listeners.

### 10. Handling Challenging Conversations:

Navigating difficult conversations can be daunting, but introverted entrepreneurs can approach them with empathy, active listening, and a focus on finding solutions rather than assigning blame.

11. The Power of Silence:

Silence is a potent tool in communication. Introverted entrepreneurs can use strategic pauses to emphasize key points, allow time for reflection, and create a sense of anticipation in their audience.

12. Seeking Feedback and Growth:

Introverted entrepreneurs should actively seek feedback on their communication skills and embrace opportunities for growth. Constructive criticism enables them to refine their approach and continually improve.

Conclusion:

The art of effective communication is an ongoing journey that requires introspection, practice, and a commitment to growth. By recognizing their innate strengths, introverted entrepreneurs can communicate with impact, influence others with authenticity, and forge meaningful connections that drive personal and professional success. Embracing public speaking, storytelling, empathetic listening, and non-verbal communication empowers introverted entrepreneurs to engage and inspire their audiences, fostering positive change and leaving a lasting impact on those they encounter. As they master the art of effective communication, introverted entrepreneurs unlock the gateway to leadership, collaboration, and the realization of their visions.

# CHAPTER 8: BUILDING CONFIDENCE: UNLEASHING YOUR QUIET INNER BOLDNESS

Introduction:

Confidence is a fundamental aspect of personal and professional growth, empowering individuals to take on challenges, make decisions, and pursue their goals with conviction. In this chapter, we explore the journey of building confidence as an introverted entrepreneur. By embracing their quiet inner boldness and recognizing their unique strengths, introverts can overcome self-doubt, unlock their full potential, and navigate their entrepreneurial journey with courage and self-assurance.

1. Understanding the Nature of Confidence:

Confidence is not an inherent trait but a skill that can be developed over time. Introverted entrepreneurs can recognize that confidence is not synonymous with extroversion, and they possess unique qualities that contribute to their quiet inner boldness.

2. Embracing Vulnerability:

Building confidence starts with embracing vulnerability and acknowledging that it is natural to experience self-doubt and fear. By accepting vulnerability as part of the growth process, introverts can approach challenges with greater resilience.

3. Setting Meaningful Goals:

Confidence flourishes when introverted entrepreneurs set meaningful and achievable goals aligned with their passions and values. Breaking down larger objectives into smaller milestones provides a sense of accomplishment and motivates continued progress.

4. Celebrating Past Achievements:

Reflecting on past accomplishments reinforces a sense of capability and serves as a reminder of the introverted entrepreneur's past successes. This acknowledgment reinforces self-belief and bolsters confidence for future endeavours.

5. Embracing a Growth Mindset:

A growth mindset, which views challenges as opportunities for learning and growth, is essential for building confidence. Introverted entrepreneurs can adopt this mindset to view setbacks as stepping stones towards improvement.

6. Challenging Limiting Beliefs:

Limiting beliefs can hinder confidence and hold introverted entrepreneurs back from pursuing their aspirations. By challenging and reframing these beliefs, they open themselves up to new possibilities and untapped potential.

7. Cultivating Self-Compassion:

Practicing self-compassion involves being kind to oneself and recognizing that everyone experiences setbacks and imperfections. By treating themselves with understanding and forgiveness, introverted entrepreneurs nurture their confidence and self-worth.

8. Seeking Supportive Networks:

Confidence thrives in a supportive environment. Introverted entrepreneurs can seek out networks that value and encourage their unique contributions, providing validation and empowerment.

9. Embracing Continuous Learning:

Confidence grows through knowledge and expertise. By continuously learning and expanding their skills, introverted entrepreneurs gain the confidence to tackle new challenges and innovate in their field.

10. Practicing Visualization:

Visualization is a powerful tool for building confidence. Introverted entrepreneurs can imagine themselves succeeding in their endeavours, rehearsing positive outcomes in their minds before taking action.

### 11. Stepping Out of Comfort Zones:

Confidence blossoms when introverted entrepreneurs embrace discomfort and step outside of their comfort zones. Each new experience builds resilience and reinforces their inner boldness.

### 12. Celebrating Self-Expression:

Introverted entrepreneurs can unleash their quiet inner boldness by celebrating their unique self-expression. Embracing their individuality and authentic voice allows them to stand out and make a memorable impact.

Conclusion:

Building confidence as an introverted entrepreneur is a transformative journey that requires self-compassion, vulnerability, and a commitment to continuous growth. Embracing their quiet inner boldness empowers introverted individuals to take on challenges with courage, embrace discomfort, and pursue their dreams with unwavering determination. By setting meaningful goals, challenging limiting beliefs, and surrounding themselves with supportive networks, introverted entrepreneurs create a fertile ground for their confidence to flourish. As they unlock their full potential, they inspire others to embrace their introverted strengths and unleash their own inner boldness. With newfound confidence, introverted entrepreneurs can navigate their entrepreneurial journey with grace, authenticity, and a quiet but powerful sense of self-assurance.

# CHAPTER 9: TIME MANAGEMENT FOR INTROVERTS: PRODUCTIVITY WITH PURPOSE

Introduction:

Time management is a critical skill for success in the fast-paced world of entrepreneurship. For introverted entrepreneurs, effective time management goes beyond maximizing productivity; it involves aligning tasks with personal values, preserving energy, and maintaining a sense of purpose. In this chapter, we explore the art of time management for introverts, providing strategies to optimize productivity while honouring their unique needs and strengths.

1. Embracing Introverted Energy Patterns:

Introverts have distinct energy patterns that influence their productivity. Recognizing peak times of focus and creativity, as well as moments of rest and recharge, enables introverted entrepreneurs to structure their days accordingly.

2. Identifying Priorities and Values:

Time management starts with clarity about priorities and values. Introverted entrepreneurs can identify their most significant goals and ensure that their daily activities align with their overarching vision.

3. The Power of Deep Work:

Introverts thrive in deep work – focused and uninterrupted periods of concentration. Creating dedicated blocks of time for deep work allows introverted entrepreneurs to tackle complex tasks and make significant progress.

4. Utilizing Time Blocking:

Time blocking involves scheduling specific tasks or activities into designated time slots. For introverted entrepreneurs, this method provides structure, minimizes decision fatigue, and ensures a balance between work and rest.

5. Leveraging Digital Tools:

Digital productivity tools can be valuable assets for introverted entrepreneurs. Task management apps, calendar tools, and note-taking software facilitate organization and efficiency in daily operations.

6. Planning for Rest and Recovery:

Rest and recovery are essential for introverted entrepreneurs to maintain productivity and prevent burnout. Scheduling downtime and self-care activities fosters overall well-being and rejuvenates creative energy.

7. Avoiding Overcommitment:

Introverts may feel pressured to say yes to every opportunity, leading to overcommitment and exhaustion. Learning to say no to non-essential tasks allows them to focus on activities that align with their goals.

8. Creating Introvert-Friendly Workspaces:

The physical environment significantly impacts productivity for introverts. Designing workspaces with minimal distractions, comfortable furniture, and natural lighting enhances focus and concentration.

9. Emphasizing Single-Tasking:

Introverted entrepreneurs excel in single-tasking, focusing on one activity at a time. This approach enhances concentration, attention to detail, and the quality of work produced.

10. The Art of Saying No:

Saying no is a valuable skill for introverted entrepreneurs. By setting boundaries and declining distractions, they protect their time and preserve energy for essential tasks.

## 11. Managing Digital Overload:

Introverts may feel overwhelmed by constant digital communication. Implementing strategies to manage email, social media, and other digital distractions allows for increased productivity and mental clarity.

## 12. Reflecting and Refining:

Effective time management is an ongoing process. Regularly reflecting on accomplishments, challenges, and lessons learned helps introverted entrepreneurs refine their time management strategies for continuous improvement.

Conclusion:

Time management for introverted entrepreneurs is not about squeezing every minute of the day with tasks but rather aligning actions with purpose and values. By recognizing energy patterns, setting priorities, and emphasizing deep work, introverted entrepreneurs can maximize productivity while preserving their well-being. The art of time management for introverts allows them to craft a purpose-driven schedule, maintain a sense of balance, and navigate their entrepreneurial journey with intention and fulfillment. By embracing their introverted strengths and honouring their unique needs, introverted entrepreneurs can achieve productivity with purpose, leaving a lasting impact on their business, their community, and themselves.

# CHAPTER 10: OVERCOMING INTROVERTED CHALLENGES: TURNING WEAKNESSES INTO STRENGTHS

Introduction:

While introverted entrepreneurs possess unique strengths, they may also face specific challenges in the dynamic world of business. However, these challenges can be transformative opportunities for growth. In this chapter, we explore how introverted individuals can overcome their challenges and transform perceived weaknesses into strengths. By embracing their introversion, practicing self-awareness, and cultivating resilience, introverted entrepreneurs can navigate their journey with confidence and create a lasting impact.

1. Embracing Introversion with Pride:

The first step in overcoming challenges is embracing introversion as a source of strength, not weakness. By celebrating their unique traits, introverted entrepreneurs gain the confidence to tackle challenges head-on.

2. Navigating Networking and Social Situations:

Networking and socializing can be daunting for introverts, but by focusing on meaningful connections and setting realistic goals, they can approach these situations with intention and authenticity.

3. Speaking Up and Asserting Ideas:

Introverted entrepreneurs may struggle with speaking up in group settings. Through deliberate practice, cultivating self-confidence, and recognizing the value of their ideas, they can assert themselves effectively.

4. Managing Stress and Overwhelm:

Introverts can become easily overwhelmed in fast-paced and crowded environments. Implementing stress management techniques, setting boundaries, and prioritizing self-care are essential for maintaining resilience.

5. Dealing with Public Speaking Anxiety:

Public speaking anxiety is common for introverts, but it can be managed through preparation, practice, and reframing nerves as excitement. Engaging in smaller speaking opportunities can also build confidence over time.

6. Balancing Solitude and Collaboration:

Finding the right balance between solitude and collaboration is key for introverted entrepreneurs. Embracing both modes allow them to leverage deep thinking and creativity while fostering teamwork and innovation.

7. Advocating for Introverted Needs:

Introverted entrepreneurs must advocate for their needs in the workplace. This may involve requesting quiet spaces, flexible working arrangements, or alternative communication methods that align with their preferences.

8. Building Resilience in the Face of Rejection:

Rejection is an inherent part of entrepreneurship. Introverts can build resilience by reframing failure as an opportunity for growth and learning, and by seeking support from a supportive network.

9. Leveraging Active Listening:

Active listening is a strength of introverted individuals. By honing this skill, they can understand clients, customers, and team members better, leading to stronger relationships and improved business outcomes.

10. Cultivating Empathy and Emotional Intelligence:

Introverts often possess high levels of empathy and emotional intelligence. By leveraging these qualities, they can connect with others on a deeper level, leading to more meaningful collaborations and client relationships.

### 11. Turning Introverted Reflection into Strategy:

Introverted entrepreneurs' reflective nature can be leveraged to create thoughtful and well-considered business strategies. By taking the time for introspection, they can make informed decisions and anticipate challenges.

### 12. Building Supportive Networks:

Forming networks of like-minded individuals provides introverted entrepreneurs with a sense of belonging and a platform for mutual support. Collaborating with supportive allies enhances their ability to overcome challenges.

Conclusion:

Introverted challenges are not insurmountable obstacles but opportunities for growth and transformation. By embracing their introversion, practicing self-awareness, and cultivating resilience, introverted entrepreneurs can turn weaknesses into strengths. Embracing networking, public speaking, collaboration, and assertiveness becomes a journey of self-discovery and personal development. The art of overcoming introverted challenges empowers individuals to navigate their entrepreneurial path with confidence and authenticity. By celebrating their unique traits and leveraging their strengths, introverted entrepreneurs can leave a profound impact on their business, their communities, and the world at large. As they embrace their journey with pride, they inspire others to transform challenges into opportunities and unleash their full potential.

# CHAPTER 11: FINDING YOUR NICHE: CAPITALIZING ON INTROVERTED PASSIONS

Introduction:

Finding a niche is a crucial aspect of entrepreneurial success. For introverted entrepreneurs, identifying a niche that aligns with their passions and strengths can be transformative. This chapter explores the art of finding a niche and capitalizing on introverted passions. By embracing authenticity, tapping into their unique interests, and leveraging their strengths, introverted entrepreneurs can carve out a space in the market that reflects their true selves and fuels their journey to success.

1. Embracing Authenticity:

Finding a niche starts with embracing authenticity. Introverted entrepreneurs must resist the pressure to conform to popular trends and instead stay true to their passions and values.

2. Identifying Personal Passions:

Passions serve as compasses in finding a niche. Introverted entrepreneurs can reflect on their interests, hobbies, and the topics that ignite their curiosity to uncover potential niches that resonate with their hearts.

3. Recognizing Unique Strengths:

Introverted entrepreneurs possess distinctive strengths that shape their niche selection. By acknowledging their skills, expertise, and perspectives, they can identify niches where they can excel.

4. Tapping into Deep Expertise:

Deep expertise in a particular field sets introverted entrepreneurs apart. By delving into their knowledge and becoming authorities in their chosen niche, they position themselves as trusted and credible leaders.

5. Understanding Target Market Needs:

Market research is essential in finding a niche. Introverted entrepreneurs can leverage their active listening and research skills to understand the needs, pain points, and desires of their target audience.

6. Fostering Meaningful Connections:

Introverted entrepreneurs can capitalize on their ability to create meaningful connections with their audience. Engaging with customers on a personal level fosters loyalty and establishes a strong brand presence.

7. Uncovering Underserved Markets:

Introverts have a talent for introspection and seeing gaps in the market. By identifying underserved markets and unmet needs, they can create innovative solutions that stand out in a crowded marketplace.

8. Embracing Quiet Innovation:

Innovation does not always require loud and bold moves. Introverted entrepreneurs can embrace quiet innovation by carefully analysing market trends and offering unique solutions that resonate with their target audience.

9. Leveraging Content Creation:

Content creation is an effective way for introverted entrepreneurs to showcase their expertise and connect with their audience. Blogging, podcasting, and social media allow them to share their knowledge and insights.

10. Building Thought Leadership:

Thought leadership enables introverted entrepreneurs to establish authority in their niche. By sharing valuable content and insights, they position themselves as go-to experts in their field.

### 11. Scaling Mindfully:

As introverted entrepreneurs grow their business, they should do so mindfully. Scaling in a way that preserves their passion, values, and customer relationships ensures continued success.

### 12. Giving Back to the Community:

Introverted entrepreneurs can give back to their community in a way that aligns with their niche and values. By supporting causes, they are passionate about, they build a purpose-driven brand that resonates with customers.

Conclusion:

Finding a niche is a transformative process that enables introverted entrepreneurs to capitalize on their passions and strengths. Embracing authenticity, recognizing unique expertise, and tapping into market needs allow them to carve out a space in the market that reflects their true selves. By building meaningful connections, fostering innovation, and offering valuable content, introverted entrepreneurs establish themselves as thought leaders in their niche. As they scale their business, they do so mindfully, preserving their passion and customer relationships. By giving back to their community, they create a purpose-driven brand that leaves a positive impact on the world. The art of finding a niche and capitalizing on introverted passions allows introverted entrepreneurs to thrive and succeed in the entrepreneurial landscape, leaving a lasting legacy that aligns with their authentic selves and fulfills their greatest aspirations.

# CHAPTER 12: THE INTROVERT'S GUIDE TO PUBLIC SPEAKING: OWNING THE STAGE

Introduction:

Public speaking is a powerful tool for communication and influence, yet it can be a source of anxiety for introverted individuals. However, with the right approach and preparation, introverted entrepreneurs can master public speaking and make a lasting impact on their audience. In this chapter, we explore the art of public speaking for introverts, offering practical strategies to build confidence, deliver compelling presentations, and authentically connect with the audience.

1. Recognizing the Power of Authenticity:

Introverted individuals must recognize that authenticity is the key to successful public speaking. Embracing their unique communication style and personality allows them to connect with the audience genuinely.

2. Cultivating a Growth Mindset:

A growth mindset is fundamental to mastering public speaking. Introverted entrepreneurs can view public speaking as a skill to develop, rather than a fixed trait, enabling them to embrace learning and improvement.

3. Preparing with Precision:

Effective preparation is essential for introverted speakers. By thoroughly researching their topic, structuring their content, and practicing their delivery, they gain the confidence needed to own the stage.

4. Embracing Nervous Energy:

Feeling nervous before speaking is normal, even for introverts. Embracing nervous energy and transforming it into enthusiasm helps introverted speakers channel their emotions positively.

5.  Utilizing Visualization Techniques:

Introverted speakers can use visualization techniques to mentally rehearse their presentations. Imagining themselves delivering a successful speech fosters confidence and reduces anxiety.

6.  Engaging the Audience Thoughtfully:

Introverted speakers excel at engaging the audience thoughtfully. They can incorporate interactive elements, ask thought-provoking questions, and foster meaningful dialogue, creating a memorable experience.

7.  The Power of Storytelling:

Storytelling is a potent tool for introverted speakers to captivate their audience. Crafting authentic and relatable narratives enhances connection and helps convey complex ideas effectively.

8.  Leveraging Visual Aids:

Visual aids, such as slides or props, enhance the impact of a presentation. Introverted speakers can use visual aids strategically to reinforce key points and maintain audience engagement.

9.  Practicing the Art of Pausing:

Pausing strategically during a speech adds emphasis and allows introverted speakers to gather their thoughts. Embracing moments of silence conveys confidence and fosters a sense of anticipation.

10. Handling Q&A Sessions:

Q&A sessions can be challenging for introverted speakers, but by actively listening to questions, staying composed, and providing thoughtful responses, they can navigate these sessions effectively.

11. Seeking Support and Feedback:

Introverted speakers should seek support and feedback from trusted allies. Constructive criticism helps them refine their speaking skills and gain a fresh perspective on their presentations.

12. Reflecting and Growing:

Public speaking is a continuous journey of growth. Introverted speakers can reflect on their experiences, celebrate their progress, and set new goals for future speaking engagements.

Conclusion:

The introvert's guide to public speaking empowers introverted entrepreneurs to step onto the stage with confidence, authenticity, and impact. By embracing their unique communication style, cultivating a growth mindset, and preparing diligently, introverted speakers can captivate their audience and leave a lasting impression. Utilizing visualization, storytelling, and engaging the audience thoughtfully creates memorable presentations that resonate with listeners. Public speaking becomes an opportunity for introverted entrepreneurs to connect with their audience genuinely, share their knowledge and insights, and inspire positive change. As they seek support, embrace feedback, and continuously grow, introverted speakers unlock their full potential and own the stage with grace and conviction. The art of public speaking for introverts transforms anxiety into enthusiasm, fear into empowerment, and silence into a powerful voice that resonates with audiences far and wide.

# CHAPTER 13: DEVELOPING EMOTIONAL INTELLIGENCE: ENHANCING BUSINESS RELATIONSHIPS

Introduction:

Emotional intelligence (EI) is a critical skill for success in business and entrepreneurship. For introverted entrepreneurs, mastering emotional intelligence allows them to navigate interpersonal dynamics with finesse, build meaningful connections, and foster productive collaborations. In this chapter, we delve into the art of developing emotional intelligence, providing insights and strategies for introverts to enhance their understanding of emotions, communicate effectively, and cultivate positive relationships in the business world.

1. Understanding Emotional Intelligence:

Emotional intelligence involves recognizing, understanding, and managing both one's own emotions and the emotions of others. Introverted entrepreneurs can embrace the value of EI in building strong business relationships.

2. Embracing Empathy:

Empathy is a cornerstone of emotional intelligence. Introverted entrepreneurs can cultivate empathy by actively listening, putting themselves in others' shoes, and acknowledging different perspectives.

3. Honing Self-Awareness:

Self-awareness is crucial for developing emotional intelligence. Introverted entrepreneurs can engage in introspection, identify their emotions, and recognize how their feelings influence their actions and decisions.

4. Managing Emotions Effectively:

Introverted entrepreneurs should learn to manage their emotions constructively. Techniques such as mindfulness, deep breathing, and emotional self-regulation empower them to respond rather than react in challenging situations.

5. Recognizing Non-Verbal Cues:

Introverts excel at picking up on non-verbal cues. Understanding body language, facial expressions, and vocal tones helps them read between the lines and grasp the underlying emotions of others.

6. Building Resilience:

Emotional intelligence fosters resilience, enabling introverted entrepreneurs to bounce back from setbacks and face adversity with courage. Resilience empowers them to stay focused on their goals despite challenges.

7. Communicating Emotions Effectively:

Communicating emotions clearly and assertively is a skill introverted entrepreneurs can develop. Expressing emotions in a constructive manner fosters open communication and strengthens business relationships.

8. Conflict Resolution:

Emotional intelligence equips introverted entrepreneurs with the tools to handle conflicts with tact and empathy. Engaging in constructive dialogue and seeking win-win solutions promotes harmonious business relationships.

9. Practicing Active Listening:

Introverted entrepreneurs' inclination towards active listening enhances emotional intelligence. By being fully present and engaged in conversations, they demonstrate respect and build rapport with others.

### 10. Cultivating Emotional Awareness in Teams:

When leading a team, introverted entrepreneurs can foster emotional awareness among team members. Encouraging open communication and recognizing emotions in the workplace promotes a positive and supportive team culture.

### 11. Responding to Criticism:

Emotionally intelligent introverts respond to criticism with grace and humility. They view feedback as an opportunity for growth and use it to improve their skills and performance.

### 12. Developing Trust and Authenticity:

Building trust is vital in business relationships. Introverted entrepreneurs can develop trust by being authentic, consistent, and reliable, aligning their actions with their words.

Conclusion:

Developing emotional intelligence is a transformative journey that allows introverted entrepreneurs to enhance their business relationships significantly. By embracing empathy, honing self-awareness, and managing emotions effectively, they create a positive and harmonious work environment. Understanding non-verbal cues, communicating emotions, and resolving conflicts with empathy fosters strong connections with team members, clients, and partners. Emotional intelligence enables introverted entrepreneurs to navigate interpersonal dynamics with finesse, promote open communication, and build trust with authenticity. As they cultivate emotional intelligence, they empower themselves to lead with empathy, collaborate with compassion, and create a supportive business ecosystem. The art of developing emotional intelligence enhances business relationships and leaves a lasting impact, elevating the success and fulfillment of introverted entrepreneurs in their entrepreneurial journey.

# CHAPTER 14: INTROVERT-FRIENDLY MARKETING: STRATEGIES FOR SUCCESS

Introduction:

Marketing is an essential aspect of entrepreneurship, but traditional marketing methods can be overwhelming and exhausting for introverted entrepreneurs. In this chapter, we explore the concept of introvert-friendly marketing, providing strategies and techniques that align with introverted strengths and preferences. By embracing authenticity, leveraging digital platforms, and focusing on meaningful connections, introverted entrepreneurs can create successful marketing campaigns that resonate with their target audience and drive business growth.

1. Embracing Authenticity in Marketing:

Authenticity is the foundation of introvert-friendly marketing. By staying true to their values, beliefs, and personality, introverted entrepreneurs create a genuine and trustworthy brand identity that resonates with customers.

2. Tapping into Introverted Creativity:

Introverted entrepreneurs possess a wealth of creativity. By leveraging their introspective nature and imagination, they can craft unique and compelling marketing campaigns that stand out in the crowded marketplace.

3. Utilizing Digital Platforms:

Digital marketing provides a comfortable and effective space for introverted entrepreneurs to reach their audience. Leveraging social media, content marketing, and email campaigns allows for targeted and engaging marketing efforts.

4. Focusing on Niche Marketing:

Niche marketing aligns with introverted strengths. By identifying a specific target audience and tailoring marketing messages to their needs and preferences, introverted entrepreneurs can foster meaningful connections.

### 5. Embracing Thought Leadership:

Introverted entrepreneurs can establish themselves as thought leaders in their industry. Sharing valuable insights, expertise, and knowledge through blogs, webinars, and podcasts enhances credibility and authority.

### 6. Nurturing Meaningful Customer Relationships:

Building authentic and meaningful relationships with customers is a hallmark of introvert-friendly marketing. Engaging in one-on-one conversations, responding to inquiries, and valuing customer feedback fosters loyalty and trust.

### 7. Leveraging Storytelling:

Storytelling is a powerful tool in introvert-friendly marketing. Sharing personal stories, customer success stories, and the brand's journey humanizes the business and creates emotional connections.

### 8. Utilizing Introverted Listening Skills:

Introverted entrepreneurs' listening skills are invaluable in marketing. By actively listening to customers' feedback, needs, and pain points, they can tailor marketing messages to address specific concerns.

### 9. Leveraging Video Content:

Video content is an effective medium for introverted entrepreneurs to share their expertise and connect with their audience. Pre-recorded videos and live streams enable authentic communication and foster engagement.

### 10. Implementing Thoughtful Networking:

Networking can be overwhelming for introverted entrepreneurs, but they can implement thoughtful networking strategies.

Attending small, focused events and building genuine connections over time facilitate meaningful partnerships.

11. Focusing on Quality over Quantity:

Introvert-friendly marketing prioritizes quality over quantity. Rather than bombarding the audience with constant messages, introverted entrepreneurs focus on delivering valuable and impactful content.

12. Honouring Rest and Recharge:

Marketing efforts can be draining for introverts. By honouring rest and recharge, they maintain their energy levels, prevent burnout, and ensure sustained creativity and enthusiasm.

Conclusion:

Introvert-friendly marketing is a powerful approach that enables introverted entrepreneurs to thrive in the world of entrepreneurship. By embracing authenticity, leveraging digital platforms, and focusing on meaningful connections, they create marketing campaigns that resonate with their audience and drive business success. Tapping into introverted creativity, storytelling, and listening skills allows for unique and engaging marketing efforts. Embracing thought leadership, nurturing customer relationships, and implementing thoughtful networking strategies build a brand identity that reflects the values and personality of the introverted entrepreneur. By focusing on quality over quantity and honouring rest and recharge, they sustain their energy and enthusiasm for marketing efforts. The art of introvert-friendly marketing creates a positive impact, enabling introverted entrepreneurs to connect with their audience authentically, drive business growth, and leave a lasting impression in the hearts and minds of their customers.

# CHAPTER 15: MASTERING THE ART OF LISTENING: THE INTROVERT'S SUPERPOWER

Introduction:

Listening is a potent skill that introverted entrepreneurs naturally excel at. In a world filled with noise and constant communication, the art of listening becomes a superpower that sets introverts apart. In this chapter, we explore the significance of mastering the art of listening for introverts. By harnessing their innate abilities to listen actively, empathetically, and with genuine interest, introverted entrepreneurs can forge deeper connections, foster collaboration, and drive meaningful change in their personal and professional lives.

1. Understanding the Power of Listening:

Listening goes beyond merely hearing words; it involves fully understanding and engaging with the speaker's message and emotions. Introverted entrepreneurs can appreciate the power of listening in cultivating stronger relationships and building trust.

2. Embracing Active Listening:

Active listening is a core strength of introverts. By giving their full attention, maintaining eye contact, and offering verbal and non-verbal cues, they demonstrate respect and create a safe space for others to express themselves.

3. Nurturing Empathy through Listening:

Empathy is a natural extension of active listening for introverted entrepreneurs. By understanding others' emotions and perspectives, they form deeper connections and strengthen their emotional intelligence.

4. Overcoming the Urge to Speak:

Introverts may struggle with the urge to interject or share their own experiences while listening. By practicing patience and focusing on the speaker, they develop a deeper understanding of others' thoughts and feelings.

### 5. Fostering Effective Communication:

Effective communication starts with attentive listening. Introverted entrepreneurs can ensure that their messages are better received by first understanding their audience's needs and concerns through active listening.

### 6. Gaining Insights and Learning:

Listening allows introverted entrepreneurs to gain valuable insights and knowledge from others. By seeking to understand diverse viewpoints, they continuously expand their understanding and expertise.

### 7. Enhancing Decision-Making:

Active listening enhances decision-making for introverted entrepreneurs. By carefully considering different perspectives and information, they make well-informed choices that align with their goals and values.

### 8. Creating a Supportive Environment:

Introverted entrepreneurs can foster a supportive and collaborative environment by being approachable listeners. Their empathetic listening style encourages open communication and promotes teamwork.

### 9. Building Trust and Rapport:

Effective listening builds trust and rapport with clients, team members, and partners. By genuinely caring about others' opinions and needs, introverted entrepreneurs create strong and lasting relationships.

### 10. Leveraging Listening in Negotiations:

Listening plays a vital role in successful negotiations. Introverted entrepreneurs can identify the other party's interests and concerns through attentive listening, leading to mutually beneficial agreements.

### 11. Promoting Conflict Resolution:

Active listening is a cornerstone of conflict resolution. By understanding the underlying emotions and issues, introverted entrepreneurs can facilitate constructive dialogues and find amicable solutions.

### 12. Unleashing the Power of Silence:

Silence is an essential aspect of effective listening. Introverted entrepreneurs can use strategic pauses to encourage others to share more deeply and reflect on their thoughts.

Conclusion:

Mastering the art of listening is a transformative skill that elevates introverted entrepreneurs in both their personal and professional lives. By embracing active listening, nurturing empathy, and overcoming the urge to speak, introverted entrepreneurs create a safe and supportive space for others to express themselves. Effective communication, enhanced decision-making, and a supportive environment become natural outcomes of their listening prowess. Building trust, fostering collaboration, and promoting conflict resolution are among the many benefits introverted entrepreneurs gain from their superpower of listening. As they harness this skill, introverted entrepreneurs forge meaningful connections, drive positive change, and leave a lasting impact on those they encounter. The art of mastering the art of listening transforms introverts into powerful communicators, compassionate leaders, and agents of change, making their mark on the world with their attentive and empathetic presence.

# CHAPTER 16: NEGOTIATION SKILLS FOR INTROVERTED ENTREPRENEURS: FINDING WIN-WIN SOLUTIONS

Introduction:

Negotiation is an integral part of entrepreneurship, involving the art of finding mutually beneficial solutions in business dealings. For introverted entrepreneurs, who often prefer introspection and thoughtful communication, mastering negotiation skills can be transformative. In this chapter, we explore the significance of negotiation for introverted entrepreneurs, offering strategies to enhance their communication, foster empathy, and create win-win outcomes that build lasting business relationships.

1. Recognizing the Value of Negotiation:

Negotiation is more than haggling over terms; it is a process of collaboration and problem-solving. Introverted entrepreneurs can recognize the value of negotiation as a tool for building partnerships and achieving business objectives.

2. Cultivating a Calm and Composed Demeanour:

Introverted entrepreneurs' calm and composed demeanour is a strength in negotiations. By staying composed under pressure, they maintain clarity and focus during discussions.

3. Preparing Thoroughly:

Thorough preparation is essential for introverted negotiators. Researching the other party, clarifying goals, and anticipating potential obstacles enable them to negotiate with confidence.

4. Leveraging Active Listening:

Active listening is a crucial skill in negotiation. By truly understanding the other party's needs, interests, and concerns, introverted entrepreneurs can tailor their proposals for better outcomes.

5. Empathizing with the Other Party:

Empathy is a powerful tool in negotiation. Introverted entrepreneurs can empathize with the other party's perspective, leading to better rapport and the potential for creative solutions.

6. Embracing the Power of Silence:

Silence can be an introverted negotiator's ally. Strategic pauses allow them to reflect, gather their thoughts, and encourage the other party to share more information.

7. Focusing on Interests, Not Positions:

Introverted entrepreneurs excel at looking beyond surface demands to identify underlying interests. By focusing on interests rather than rigid positions, they open the door to more flexible and satisfying agreements.

8. Communicating Clearly and Assertively:

Effective communication is key in negotiation. Introverted entrepreneurs can communicate their ideas, needs, and boundaries clearly and assertively to ensure they are understood and respected.

9. Managing Emotions Effectively:

Negotiations can be emotionally charged, but introverted entrepreneurs can manage their emotions effectively. By staying composed and refraining from making impulsive decisions, they maintain control over the negotiation process.

10. Seeking Win-Win Solutions:

The ultimate goal in negotiation is to find win-win solutions. Introverted entrepreneurs can create outcomes that benefit all parties involved, fostering a sense of cooperation and long-term business relationships.

### 11. Handling Conflict Constructively:

Conflict is a natural part of negotiation, but introverted entrepreneurs can handle it constructively. By maintaining a cooperative attitude and seeking common ground, they turn conflicts into opportunities for resolution.

### 12. Building Long-Term Relationships:

Negotiation is not just about closing a deal; it's about building lasting relationships. Introverted entrepreneurs can prioritize relationship-building, leading to future collaborations and referrals.

Conclusion:

Negotiation skills are a powerful asset for introverted entrepreneurs, enabling them to navigate business dealings with confidence and integrity. By recognizing the value of negotiation, cultivating a composed demeanour, and preparing thoroughly, they lay the foundation for successful negotiations. Leveraging active listening, empathy, and the power of silence allows introverted entrepreneurs to truly understand the other party and create win-win outcomes. Focusing on interests, communicating assertively, and managing emotions effectively ensure a constructive negotiation process. Seeking win-win solutions and handling conflict constructively fosters a sense of collaboration and trust. The art of negotiation empowers introverted entrepreneurs to build meaningful and long-term business relationships, positioning them as respected and effective communicators in the entrepreneurial landscape. By finding balance in their negotiation style and embracing their strengths, introverted entrepreneurs excel in finding win-win solutions that advance their business objectives while fostering positive connections with others.

# CHAPTER 17: MANAGING STRESS AND BURNOUT: BALANCING ENTREPRENEURSHIP AND WELL-BEING

Introduction:

Entrepreneurship is a rewarding journey, but it can also be demanding and overwhelming, leading to stress and burnout. For introverted entrepreneurs, who may need more time alone to recharge, managing stress and maintaining well-being is crucial. In this chapter, we explore the importance of stress management and self-care for introverted entrepreneurs. By understanding the signs of stress, implementing coping strategies, and finding a balance between work and self-care, introverted entrepreneurs can thrive in their entrepreneurial pursuits while safeguarding their physical and mental well-being.

1.  Recognizing the Impact of Stress on Well-being:

Introverted entrepreneurs must acknowledge the impact of stress on their physical and mental health. Understanding the signs and symptoms of stress empowers them to take proactive measures.

2.  Embracing Self-Care as a Priority:

Self-care is not a luxury; it is an essential aspect of maintaining well-being. Introverted entrepreneurs can embrace self-care as a priority, incorporating it into their daily routines to replenish their energy and resilience.

3.  Setting Boundaries for Work-Life Integration:

Work-life integration is a challenge for introverted entrepreneurs who may struggle with separating work and personal time. By setting clear boundaries and sticking to them, they prevent burnout and achieve a better work-life balance.

4. Utilizing Mindfulness and Meditation:

Mindfulness and meditation are effective tools for introverted entrepreneurs to reduce stress and increase self-awareness. Engaging in mindfulness practices promotes mental clarity and emotional well-being.

5. Incorporating Relaxation Techniques:

Introverted entrepreneurs can benefit from relaxation techniques, such as deep breathing exercises, progressive muscle relaxation, and nature walks, to alleviate stress and promote relaxation.

6. Prioritizing Sleep:

Quality sleep is vital for introverted entrepreneurs to recharge and maintain optimal performance. Prioritizing sleep hygiene and creating a restful sleep environment supports overall well-being.

7. Seeking Support Networks:

Introverted entrepreneurs should seek support from like-minded individuals or professional networks. Sharing experiences and challenges with others fosters a sense of camaraderie and reduces feelings of isolation.

8. Managing Workload and Time:

Overcommitment and poor time management can contribute to stress. Introverted entrepreneurs can manage their workload and time effectively, focusing on priorities and delegating tasks when needed.

9. Creating an Introvert-Friendly Work Environment:

Designing a work environment that aligns with introverted preferences enhances well-being. Providing quiet spaces for concentration and limiting unnecessary interruptions support productivity and mental health.

10. Incorporating Regular Breaks:

Introverted entrepreneurs benefit from taking regular breaks during work hours. Short breaks allow them to recharge, refocus, and return to tasks with renewed energy and creativity.

11. Adopting a Healthy Lifestyle:

A healthy lifestyle contributes to overall well-being. Introverted entrepreneurs can prioritize regular physical activity, a balanced diet, and other healthy habits to enhance their resilience to stress.

12. Recognizing the Need for Professional Help:

In some cases, stress and burnout may require professional intervention. Introverted entrepreneurs should recognize when they need help and seek support from mental health professionals.

Conclusion:

Managing stress and maintaining well-being is a critical aspect of entrepreneurship for introverted individuals. By recognizing the impact of stress, embracing self-care, and setting boundaries, they safeguard their physical and mental health. Incorporating mindfulness, relaxation techniques, and regular breaks allows them to recharge and reduce the effects of stress. Prioritizing sleep, seeking support networks, and managing workload and time contribute to a balanced and fulfilling entrepreneurial journey. By creating an introvert-friendly work environment and adopting a healthy lifestyle, introverted entrepreneurs enhance their resilience to stress and burnout. The art of managing stress and burnout empowers introverted entrepreneurs to achieve success while maintaining their well-being. By prioritizing self-care, seeking balance, and recognizing the importance of mental health, they create a sustainable and fulfilling entrepreneurial path. As they embrace stress management strategies and prioritize their well-being, introverted entrepreneurs foster a thriving business and a healthier, happier life.

# CHAPTER 18: THE POWER OF SOLITUDE: TAPPING INTO CREATIVITY AND INNOVATION

Introduction:

Solitude is often misunderstood as isolation, but for introverted entrepreneurs, it is a source of strength and creativity. In the fast-paced and interconnected world of business, embracing moments of solitude can be transformative. In this chapter, we explore the power of solitude for introverted entrepreneurs, understanding its role in fostering creativity, innovation, and self-discovery. By valuing solitude as a tool for deep thinking, reflection, and idea generation, introverted entrepreneurs can harness its potential to drive their businesses forward and make a lasting impact.

1. Rethinking Solitude:

Solitude is not synonymous with loneliness; it is a conscious choice to be alone and find inner peace. Introverted entrepreneurs can reframe solitude as an opportunity for growth, creativity, and self-renewal.

2. The Creative Sanctuary of Solitude:

Solitude creates a creative sanctuary for introverted entrepreneurs. Away from distractions and external noise, they can tap into their imagination and explore innovative ideas.

3. Deep Thinking and Problem-Solving:

Introverted entrepreneurs thrive in solitude when it comes to deep thinking and problem-solving. Moments of quiet contemplation allow them to analyse complex issues and devise effective solutions.

4. Embracing Introspection:

Introspection is an introvert's superpower. Through solitude, they can explore their thoughts, feelings, and aspirations, gaining deeper self-awareness and understanding.

5. Stimulating Curiosity and Learning:

Solitude fosters curiosity and a thirst for learning. Introverted entrepreneurs can explore new subjects, read, and engage in self-directed learning to expand their knowledge base.

6. Fostering Innovation:

Innovation often springs from moments of solitude. Introverted entrepreneurs can brainstorm new concepts, challenge conventional thinking, and pioneer groundbreaking solutions.

7. The Role of Solitude in Decision-Making:

Solitude plays a pivotal role in decision-making for introverted entrepreneurs. By reflecting on their values, goals, and instincts, they can make well-considered choices with confidence.

8. Enhancing Concentration and Focus:

Distractions can hinder productivity, but solitude allows introverted entrepreneurs to concentrate and focus deeply on their tasks, resulting in high-quality work.

9. Creativity through Solitude and Nature:

Nature can be a powerful backdrop for solitude, inspiring introverted entrepreneurs with its beauty and tranquillity. Spending time outdoors enhances creativity and rejuvenates the mind.

10. The Intersection of Solitude and Inspiration:

Introverted entrepreneurs find inspiration in solitude. They can explore their thoughts and experiences, leading to authentic and inspiring ideas for their businesses.

11. Balancing Solitude and Collaboration:

Solitude and collaboration are not mutually exclusive. Introverted entrepreneurs can find a balance by seeking solitude when needed and collaborating with others to bring ideas to life.

12. Cultivating a Solitude Practice:

Introverted entrepreneurs can cultivate a solitude practice that aligns with their needs and preferences. By setting aside dedicated time for reflection and creativity, they nurture their well-being and productivity.

Conclusion:

The power of solitude is a valuable asset for introverted entrepreneurs, offering them a sanctuary for creativity, innovation, and self-discovery. By embracing solitude and reframing it as a source of strength, they tap into their creative potential and gain deeper insights into their businesses and themselves. Solitude allows for deep thinking, problem-solving, and decision-making, providing clarity and focus amidst the hustle of entrepreneurship. The practice of introspection fosters self-awareness and personal growth, leading to more authentic and purpose-driven business strategies. Solitude stimulates curiosity, inspiration, and a thirst for learning, propelling introverted entrepreneurs to pioneer innovative solutions in their industries. As they balance solitude with collaboration, they create an ecosystem where creative ideas flourish, teamwork thrives, and meaningful contributions are made. The art of tapping into solitude's power enables introverted entrepreneurs to find their creative flow, develop unique business propositions, and lead with confidence and authenticity. By valuing solitude and embracing its gifts, introverted entrepreneurs forge a path of innovation and impact, leaving a lasting legacy in the entrepreneurial landscape.

# CHAPTER 19: EMBRACING CHANGE: THRIVING IN DYNAMIC BUSINESS ENVIRONMENTS

Introduction:

Change is a constant in the world of business, and for introverted entrepreneurs, navigating dynamic environments can be both challenging and rewarding. In this chapter, we explore the art of embracing change, understanding its inevitability, and leveraging it as an opportunity for growth and innovation. By developing adaptability, resilience, and a growth mindset, introverted entrepreneurs can not only survive but thrive in the face of change, leading their businesses to new heights of success and relevance.

1. Acknowledging the Nature of Change:

Change is an inherent aspect of business and life. Introverted entrepreneurs must embrace change as a natural and necessary force for progress and evolution.

2. The Power of Adaptability:

Adaptability is a crucial skill for thriving in dynamic business environments. Introverted entrepreneurs can embrace change by remaining flexible and open to new possibilities.

3. Developing a Growth Mindset:

A growth mindset empowers introverted entrepreneurs to view challenges as opportunities for learning and improvement. By seeing change as a chance to evolve, they approach it with enthusiasm.

4. Managing Fear and Uncertainty:

Change can be accompanied by fear and uncertainty. Introverted entrepreneurs can manage these emotions by focusing on what they can control and seeking support when needed.

### 5. The Role of Resilience:

Resilience is the backbone of embracing change. By bouncing back from setbacks and staying committed to their vision, introverted entrepreneurs navigate through challenges with determination.

### 6. Learning from Failures and Setbacks:

Failures and setbacks are stepping stones to success. Introverted entrepreneurs can view these experiences as valuable lessons and use them to refine their strategies.

### 7. Cultivating an Agile Business Approach:

Agility is essential for thriving in dynamic business environments. Introverted entrepreneurs can adopt an agile approach, responding quickly to changing circumstances and staying ahead of the curve.

### 8. Embracing Innovation and Creativity:

Change invites opportunities for innovation and creativity. Introverted entrepreneurs can capitalize on change by developing new ideas and solutions that meet evolving market needs.

### 9. Seeking New Perspectives:

Change often involves seeing things from a fresh perspective. Introverted entrepreneurs can engage in collaboration, seek feedback, and welcome diverse viewpoints to gain insights and inspiration.

### 10. Fostering a Culture of Continuous Improvement:

A culture of continuous improvement supports change and innovation. Introverted entrepreneurs can foster such a culture by encouraging experimentation and rewarding learning and growth.

### 11. Leading with Vision and Purpose:

In the face of change, introverted entrepreneurs can lead with a clear vision and a sense of purpose. A strong guiding force helps them and their team navigate uncertainty and stay on course.

12. Finding Balance amidst Change:

Managing change can be overwhelming, but introverted entrepreneurs can find balance by setting priorities, establishing boundaries, and taking time for self-care and reflection.

Conclusion:

Embracing change is an empowering journey that allows introverted entrepreneurs to thrive in dynamic business environments. By acknowledging the inevitability of change and cultivating adaptability, they remain agile and responsive to shifting circumstances. A growth mindset enables them to view change as an opportunity for learning and innovation, propelling their businesses forward. Resilience and the ability to learn from failures build a foundation of strength to navigate challenges with confidence. Embracing change fosters a culture of continuous improvement, where creativity and innovation flourish. Seeking new perspectives and leading with vision and purpose create a dynamic and forward-thinking business ecosystem. By finding balance amidst change and prioritizing well-being, introverted entrepreneurs ensure sustained success and fulfillment. The art of embracing change transforms introverted entrepreneurs into resilient, visionary leaders, guiding their businesses with confidence and adaptability. By embracing change as a force for growth and opportunity, introverted entrepreneurs carve a path of innovation and relevance, leaving a lasting impact in the ever-evolving world of entrepreneurship.

# CHAPTER 20: NETWORKING FOR INTROVERTS: BUILDING A SUPPORTIVE CIRCLE

Introduction:

Networking is a powerful tool for entrepreneurs, enabling them to forge connections, gain insights, and explore collaboration opportunities. However, for introverted entrepreneurs, who may feel drained by large social gatherings, traditional networking events can be overwhelming. In this chapter, we explore the art of networking for introverts, offering strategies to build a supportive circle of connections that align with their preferences and strengths. By embracing authentic networking, leveraging digital platforms, and cultivating meaningful relationships, introverted entrepreneurs can create a network that empowers them to thrive in the entrepreneurial world.

1.  Redefining Networking for Introverts:

Introverted entrepreneurs can redefine networking as a means of building authentic and meaningful connections rather than simply collecting business cards. By focusing on quality over quantity, they can create a supportive circle that enriches their entrepreneurial journey.

2.  Embracing Introverted Strengths:

Introverts possess unique strengths, such as active listening, empathy, and deep thinking, which are valuable assets in networking. Embracing these strengths allows introverted entrepreneurs to connect on a deeper level with others.

3.  Networking with Intention:

Networking with intention means seeking connections that align with one's goals and values. Introverted entrepreneurs can be strategic in their networking efforts, focusing on individuals and groups that resonate with their vision.

4. Leveraging Digital Networking:

Digital platforms offer introverted entrepreneurs an introvert-friendly space for networking. Utilizing social media, LinkedIn, and online communities allows them to connect with like-minded individuals and industry experts.

5. Participating in Small Group Events:

Large networking events can be overwhelming for introverts. Instead, they can seek out small group gatherings, workshops, or intimate meetups, where they can engage in more meaningful conversations.

6. The Power of One-on-One Networking:

One-on-one networking is a comfortable setting for introverted entrepreneurs to connect deeply with others. Scheduling coffee meetings or virtual calls enables focused and authentic conversations.

7. Cultivating Relationships Gradually:

Introverted entrepreneurs may take time to build relationships, and that is perfectly fine. Networking is about nurturing connections over time, gradually developing trust and rapport.

8. Seeking Common Interests:

Finding common interests is a natural way for introverted entrepreneurs to connect with others. Joining groups or organizations that share similar passions allows for more authentic and engaging conversations.

9. Being a Resourceful Listener:

Introverted entrepreneurs excel at being resourceful listeners. By actively engaging in conversations and asking thoughtful questions, they demonstrate genuine interest in others' experiences and insights.

### 10. Giving Value to Others:

Networking is a two-way street. Introverted entrepreneurs can give value to others by offering support, knowledge, or resources, fostering reciprocity in their relationships.

### 11. Finding an Accountability Partner:

Having an accountability partner can be beneficial for introverted entrepreneurs. A trusted individual can offer encouragement, support, and feedback, helping them stay focused on their goals.

### 12. Balancing Networking and Self-Care:

Networking can be draining for introverts, so it's crucial to balance it with self-care. Allocating time for solitude, reflection, and relaxation ensures that they maintain their energy and enthusiasm for networking.

Conclusion:

Networking for introverted entrepreneurs is a transformative process that allows them to build a supportive circle of connections that align with their values and strengths. By redefining networking as an opportunity for authentic and meaningful connections, introverted entrepreneurs create a network that enriches their entrepreneurial journey. Leveraging digital platforms, participating in small group events, and engaging in one-on-one networking enables them to connect comfortably and meaningfully with others. Cultivating relationships gradually and seeking common interests fosters deep and lasting connections. By being resourceful listeners and giving value to others, introverted entrepreneurs create a reciprocal and supportive networking dynamic. Finding an accountability partner further empowers them to stay focused on their goals and aspirations. By balancing networking with self-care, introverted entrepreneurs maintain their well-being and enthusiasm for networking efforts. The art of networking for introverts transforms them into confident and connected entrepreneurs, guiding their businesses with the support of a nurturing and empowering network. Embracing networking in a way that aligns with their preferences, introverted entrepreneurs carve a path of authenticity, collaboration, and success, leaving a lasting impact in their entrepreneurial pursuits.

# CHAPTER 21: BUILDING A PERSONAL BRAND: AUTHENTICITY AND INTROVERTED ENTREPRENEURS

Introduction:

In the modern business landscape, personal branding has become a powerful tool for entrepreneurs to establish their identity, reputation, and influence. For introverted entrepreneurs, who may prefer a more private and introspective approach, building a personal brand can seem daunting. In this chapter, we explore the art of building a personal brand for introverted entrepreneurs, emphasizing the significance of authenticity and genuine self-expression. By aligning their personal brand with their values, strengths, and unique qualities, introverted entrepreneurs can create a brand that resonates with their target audience and fosters trust and loyalty.

1. Defining Personal Branding for Introverted Entrepreneurs:

Personal branding is the process of defining one's unique identity, values, and expertise in the entrepreneurial space. For introverted entrepreneurs, personal branding is about embracing authenticity and showcasing their genuine selves to the world.

2. Embracing Introverted Strengths in Personal Branding:

Introverted entrepreneurs possess inherent strengths, such as thoughtfulness, deep insight, and authenticity, which can be powerful assets in building their personal brand.

3. Uncovering Your True Identity:

Building a personal brand starts with introspection. Introverted entrepreneurs can embark on a journey of self-discovery to uncover their true identity, values, and passions.

4. Identifying Your Unique Value Proposition:

A strong personal brand requires a clear value proposition. Introverted entrepreneurs can identify what sets them apart from others and how they can uniquely serve their target audience.

5. Communicating Your Brand Story:

Storytelling is a potent tool in personal branding. Introverted entrepreneurs can craft a compelling brand story that shares their journey, experiences, and vision, connecting with their audience on a deeper level.

6. Leveraging Authentic Content:

Authenticity is key in personal branding. Introverted entrepreneurs can create content that reflects their genuine thoughts, insights, and expertise, building trust and credibility.

7. Building Thought Leadership:

Thought leadership is an effective way for introverted entrepreneurs to establish authority in their industry. By sharing valuable insights and knowledge, they position themselves as trusted experts.

8. Navigating Social Media:

Social media can be overwhelming for introverted entrepreneurs, but it offers a platform for authentic self-expression. They can curate their online presence, engaging with their audience in a way that aligns with their personality.

9. Engaging in Meaningful Networking:

Introverted entrepreneurs can engage in networking that aligns with their values and preferences. Focusing on meaningful connections and fostering genuine relationships contributes to their personal brand.

10. Balancing Public and Private Life:

Building a personal brand requires finding a balance between public and private life. Introverted entrepreneurs can decide on the level of visibility that is comfortable for them while maintaining authenticity.

11. Showcasing Vulnerability:

Vulnerability is a strength in personal branding. By sharing challenges, failures, and growth experiences, introverted entrepreneurs create relatable and human connections with their audience.

12. Embracing Feedback and Growth:

Personal branding is an ongoing process. Introverted entrepreneurs can embrace feedback and use it as a tool for growth and refinement, evolving their personal brand over time.

Conclusion:

Building a personal brand for introverted entrepreneurs is a transformative journey that centres on authenticity and genuine self-expression. By defining their unique identity and leveraging introverted strengths, they create a personal brand that resonates with their audience. Uncovering their true identity and values allows introverted entrepreneurs to build a personal brand rooted in authenticity and purpose. Identifying their unique value proposition enables them to communicate their distinctive offerings to their target audience. Sharing their brand story through authentic content and thought leadership establishes them as credible and trustworthy entrepreneurs. Navigating social media and networking in a way that aligns with their personality fosters meaningful connections and relationships. Balancing public and private life while showcasing vulnerability creates a relatable and approachable personal brand. Embracing feedback and continuous growth ensures that their personal brand evolves and remains relevant over time. The art of building a personal brand for introverted entrepreneurs transforms them into authentic and influential thought leaders, guiding their businesses with a unique and genuine identity. By embracing personal branding as a means of self-expression and connection, introverted entrepreneurs create a lasting impact in the hearts and minds of their audience, leaving a meaningful legacy in the entrepreneurial world.

# CHAPTER 22: GOAL SETTING AND ACHIEVING: STEPPING OUT OF YOUR COMFORT ZONE

Introduction:

Goal setting is a fundamental aspect of personal and professional growth, providing a roadmap for success and fulfillment. For introverted entrepreneurs, who may be more reserved and cautious by nature, stepping out of their comfort zone to set ambitious goals can be a transformative process. In this chapter, we explore the art of goal setting and achieving for introverted entrepreneurs, emphasizing the significance of embracing discomfort and taking calculated risks. By setting bold and meaningful goals, introverted entrepreneurs can break free from self-imposed limitations and achieve remarkable success in their entrepreneurial journey.

1. Understanding the Power of Goal Setting:

Goal setting empowers introverted entrepreneurs to define their vision, clarify their objectives, and map out their path to success. Understanding the power of goal setting inspires them to dream big and reach their full potential.

2. Embracing Discomfort as a Catalyst for Growth:

Stepping out of one's comfort zone can be uncomfortable but is essential for personal growth. Introverted entrepreneurs can embrace discomfort as a catalyst for learning, resilience, and transformative experiences.

3. Setting SMART Goals:

SMART (Specific, Measurable, Achievable, Relevant, Time-bound) goals provide a clear framework for introverted entrepreneurs to create well-defined and attainable objectives.

### 4. Establishing Stretch Goals:

Stretch goals push introverted entrepreneurs beyond their perceived limits. By setting ambitious targets, they unlock untapped potential and achieve more than they ever imagined.

### 5. Breaking Goals into Manageable Steps:

Breaking larger goals into smaller, manageable steps makes them less overwhelming for introverted entrepreneurs. This approach encourages consistent progress and boosts motivation.

### 6. Cultivating a Growth Mindset:

A growth mindset is essential for achieving goals. Introverted entrepreneurs can cultivate a mindset that embraces challenges as opportunities for learning and improvement.

### 7. Overcoming Fear of Failure:

Fear of failure can hold introverted entrepreneurs back from pursuing their goals. By reframing failure as a stepping stone to success, they become more resilient and daring in their pursuits.

### 8. Seeking Accountability and Support:

Accountability and support play a vital role in goal achievement. Introverted entrepreneurs can seek an accountability partner or join a mastermind group to stay focused and encouraged.

### 9. Evaluating Progress and Adjusting Course:

Regularly assessing progress and adjusting course allows introverted entrepreneurs to stay on track and make necessary course corrections to reach their goals.

### 10. Celebrating Milestones and Achievements:

Celebrating milestones and achievements is crucial for maintaining motivation and fostering a positive mindset. Introverted entrepreneurs can acknowledge their progress, no matter how small.

### 11. Expanding Comfort Zones Gradually:

Stepping out of one's comfort zone is a gradual process.

Introverted entrepreneurs can start with smaller challenges and progressively take on more significant risks as their confidence grows.

12. Focusing on Intrinsic Motivation:

Intrinsic motivation, driven by passion and purpose, sustains introverted entrepreneurs during challenging times. By focusing on the why behind their goals, they stay committed and inspired.

Conclusion:

Goal setting and achieving is a transformative journey for introverted entrepreneurs, leading them to surpass self-imposed limitations and achieve remarkable success. By understanding the power of goal setting and embracing discomfort as a catalyst for growth, they unlock their full potential. Setting SMART and stretch goals empowers them to create well-defined objectives and aim higher than they thought possible. Breaking goals into manageable steps ensures steady progress and momentum. Cultivating a growth mindset and overcoming fear of failure instils resilience and daring in their pursuit of success. Seeking accountability and support keeps them focused and encouraged on their journey. Evaluating progress and celebrating milestones fosters motivation and a positive mindset. Expanding comfort zones gradually allows them to embrace challenges with confidence. Focusing on intrinsic motivation ensures enduring commitment and passion. The art of goal setting and achieving transforms introverted entrepreneurs into resilient and accomplished visionaries, leading their businesses with courage and determination. By stepping out of their comfort zone and pursuing bold goals, introverted entrepreneurs make a lasting impact in the entrepreneurial world, leaving behind a legacy of achievement and inspiration.

# CHAPTER 23: THE QUIET ENTREPRENEUR'S GUIDE TO TEAM BUILDING: ASSEMBLING THE RIGHT PEOPLE

Introduction:

Team building is a critical process for any entrepreneur seeking to grow their business. For quiet or introverted entrepreneurs, who may prefer working independently, assembling the right team can pose unique challenges. In this chapter, we explore the art of team building for introverted entrepreneurs, emphasizing the significance of creating a cohesive and harmonious team that complements their strengths and values. By fostering a supportive and inclusive team culture and leveraging their introverted leadership style, introverted entrepreneurs can build a high-performing team that drives their business forward.

1. Recognizing the Value of Team Building:

Team building is not just about hiring employees; it is about building a cohesive group of individuals who work together towards a common goal. Introverted entrepreneurs can recognize the value of team building as a foundation for success.

2. Identifying the Right Team Players:

Finding the right team players is crucial for introverted entrepreneurs. They can look for individuals who share their vision, values, and passion for the business.

3. Embracing Diversity and Inclusion:

Diversity and inclusion are cornerstones of effective team building. Introverted entrepreneurs can embrace diverse perspectives, backgrounds, and skills to foster creativity and innovation within their team.

4. Creating a Positive and Supportive Team Culture:

Introverted entrepreneurs can create a team culture that values open communication, mutual respect, and support. A positive and supportive culture encourages collaboration and boosts team morale.

5. Leveraging Introverted Leadership:

Introverted leadership is characterized by thoughtful decision-making and a focus on individual strengths. Introverted entrepreneurs can leverage their leadership style to guide and empower their team members.

6. Communicating Effectively:

Effective communication is essential in team building. Introverted entrepreneurs can practice active listening and ensure that their team members feel heard and valued.

7. Nurturing Professional Development:

Nurturing professional development within the team motivates team members to grow and excel in their roles. Introverted entrepreneurs can offer opportunities for skill enhancement and learning.

8. Balancing Autonomy and Collaboration:

Introverted entrepreneurs may value autonomy, but they must strike a balance with collaboration. Allowing team members to take ownership of their work while encouraging collaboration fosters a sense of empowerment.

9. Building Trust and Psychological Safety:

Trust and psychological safety are critical for team success. Introverted entrepreneurs can create a safe environment where team members feel comfortable taking risks and sharing ideas.

10. Emphasizing Team-Building Activities:

Team-building activities help strengthen relationships among team members. Introverted entrepreneurs can organize low-key and meaningful activities that align with their team's preferences.

11. Resolving Conflict Constructively:

Conflict is a natural part of team dynamics. Introverted entrepreneurs can address conflicts promptly and constructively, promoting a culture of open communication and resolution.

12. Celebrating Team Achievements:

Recognizing and celebrating team achievements fosters a positive team spirit. Introverted entrepreneurs can express gratitude and appreciation for their team's hard work and dedication.

Conclusion:

Team building is an integral aspect of business growth for introverted entrepreneurs. By recognizing the value of building a cohesive and harmonious team, they can assemble the right individuals who share their vision and passion. Embracing diversity and inclusion within the team fosters creativity and innovation. Creating a positive and supportive team culture cultivates collaboration and high morale. Leveraging their introverted leadership style empowers introverted entrepreneurs to guide and inspire their team members. Effective communication and active listening promote open dialogue and mutual understanding. Nurturing professional development within the team motivates individuals to excel in their roles. Balancing autonomy and collaboration allow team members to take ownership while fostering a sense of teamwork. Building trust and psychological safety creates an environment where team members feel valued and empowered. Emphasizing team-building activities strengthens relationships and camaraderie. Resolving conflict constructively ensures a healthy team dynamic. Celebrating team achievements and expressing appreciation for hard work boosts team morale. The art of team building for introverted entrepreneurs transforms them into effective and respected team leaders, guiding their businesses with a high-performing and cohesive team. By fostering a supportive and inclusive team culture, introverted entrepreneurs create an environment where individuals thrive, collaborate, and achieve remarkable success together. As they build a team that complements their strengths and values, introverted entrepreneurs leave a lasting impact in their business and in the lives of their team members.

# CHAPTER 24: EMBRACING INTROVERTED SALES TECHNIQUES: SELLING WITH INTEGRITY

Introduction:

Sales is an integral aspect of entrepreneurship, but for introverted entrepreneurs, who may be more reserved and averse to aggressive tactics, traditional sales approaches can feel uncomfortable and inauthentic. In this chapter, we explore the art of embracing introverted sales techniques, emphasizing the significance of selling with integrity and authenticity. By leveraging their introverted strengths, cultivating strong relationships, and focusing on customer needs, introverted entrepreneurs can transform the sales process into a genuine and value-driven experience, leading to long-term success and customer loyalty.

1. Understanding Introverted Sales Techniques:

Introverted sales techniques differ from aggressive and pushy sales tactics. Introverted entrepreneurs can understand and embrace these techniques, which are built on building genuine connections and adding value.

2. Leveraging Introverted Strengths in Sales:

Introverted entrepreneurs possess strengths such as active listening, empathy, and deep understanding, which are powerful assets in sales. Leveraging these strengths allows them to connect with customers on a deeper level.

3. Focusing on Building Relationships:

Sales for introverted entrepreneurs is not about making a quick transaction; it is about building lasting relationships with customers. By focusing on nurturing connections, they create a loyal customer base.

4. Demonstrating Empathy and Understanding:

Empathy is a crucial element of introverted sales techniques. By understanding and addressing customer needs, introverted entrepreneurs can offer personalized and relevant solutions.

5. Asking Thoughtful Questions:

Introverted entrepreneurs can ask thoughtful questions that encourage customers to share their concerns and aspirations. These questions provide valuable insights for tailoring their offerings.

6. Listening Actively and Attentively:

Active listening is a hallmark of introverted sales techniques. By giving customers their full attention and understanding their perspectives, introverted entrepreneurs build trust and rapport.

7. Presenting Solutions with Integrity:

Selling with integrity means offering genuine solutions that align with customer needs. Introverted entrepreneurs can present their products or services honestly, avoiding exaggeration or manipulation.

8. Avoiding High-Pressure Tactics:

High-pressure sales tactics do not align with introverted sales techniques. Introverted entrepreneurs can avoid such tactics and respect their customers' decisions and boundaries.

9. Building a Value Proposition:

Creating a strong value proposition is essential for introverted entrepreneurs. By demonstrating the unique value of their offerings, they differentiate themselves from competitors.

10. Communicating Confidence and Passion:

Introverted entrepreneurs can communicate confidence and passion for their products or services in a genuine and understated manner. Authentic enthusiasm inspires trust in customers.

## 11. Using Storytelling as a Sales Tool:

Storytelling is an effective sales tool for introverted entrepreneurs. By sharing success stories or testimonials, they demonstrate how their offerings have made a positive impact on others.

## 12. Following Up with Care:

Following up with customers demonstrates commitment and care. Introverted entrepreneurs can follow up in a personalized and thoughtful manner, reinforcing their dedication to customer satisfaction.

Conclusion:

Embracing introverted sales techniques transforms the sales process for introverted entrepreneurs, enabling them to sell with integrity and authenticity. By understanding and leveraging their introverted strengths, they build genuine connections with customers. Focusing on building relationships rather than making quick transactions creates a loyal and satisfied customer base. Demonstrating empathy, asking thoughtful questions, and actively listening allow them to understand customer needs and offer personalized solutions. Selling with integrity means presenting products or services honestly and avoiding high-pressure tactics. Building a strong value proposition differentiates introverted entrepreneurs from competitors. Communicating confidence and passion in a genuine manner inspires customer trust. Using storytelling as a sales tool engages customers and showcases the positive impact of their offerings. Following up with care demonstrates commitment to customer satisfaction. The art of embracing introverted sales techniques transforms introverted entrepreneurs into trusted and respected sales professionals, leading their businesses with integrity and authenticity. By selling with integrity and adding value to their customers' lives, introverted entrepreneurs create a lasting impact in their industry, earning customer loyalty and success.

As they embrace introverted sales techniques, introverted entrepreneurs prove that genuine connections and authentic interactions are the foundation of sustainable and meaningful business growth.

# CHAPTER 25: OVERCOMING FEAR OF PUBLIC PERCEPTION: OWNING YOUR JOURNEY

Introduction:

The fear of public perception is a common challenge faced by many entrepreneurs, including introverted entrepreneurs. This fear can stem from concerns about judgment, criticism, or feeling like an imposter in the public eye. In this chapter, we explore the art of overcoming the fear of public perception for introverted entrepreneurs, emphasizing the significance of embracing their unique journey and authenticity. By cultivating self-confidence, reframing negative thoughts, and focusing on their purpose, introverted entrepreneurs can break free from the shackles of public perception and confidently own their entrepreneurial journey.

1. Understanding the Fear of Public Perception:

The fear of public perception arises from the worry about how others view and judge us. Introverted entrepreneurs can recognize this fear as a natural part of the entrepreneurial journey and acknowledge its impact on their mindset.

2. Embracing Your Unique Journey:

Every entrepreneur's journey is unique, and introverted entrepreneurs need to embrace theirs without comparing themselves to others. Recognizing their individuality and the value they bring to the table fosters self-confidence.

3. Cultivating Self-Confidence:

Confidence is the antidote to the fear of public perception. Introverted entrepreneurs can cultivate self-confidence by celebrating their achievements, acknowledging their strengths, and accepting their vulnerabilities.

4.  Reframing Negative Thoughts:

Negative thoughts and self-doubt can perpetuate the fear of public perception. Introverted entrepreneurs can challenge and reframe these thoughts, replacing them with positive affirmations and self-empowering beliefs.

5.  Accepting Constructive Feedback:

Feedback is an essential aspect of personal and professional growth. Introverted entrepreneurs can learn to accept constructive feedback gracefully, viewing it as an opportunity for improvement.

6.  Focusing on Purpose and Impact:

Keeping focus on their purpose and the impact they want to make allows introverted entrepreneurs to shift their attention away from public perception. Aligning their actions with their mission brings clarity and direction.

7.  Recognizing the Power of Vulnerability:

Vulnerability is a strength, not a weakness. Introverted entrepreneurs can recognize that sharing their struggles and imperfections fosters authentic connections with their audience.

8.  Building a Supportive Network:

Surrounding oneself with a supportive network of friends, mentors, and like-minded individuals provides encouragement and reassurance. A supportive network helps introverted entrepreneurs navigate challenges and stay true to their journey.

9.  Practicing Mindfulness and Resilience:

Mindfulness and resilience are essential tools for overcoming the fear of public perception. By staying present and adaptable, introverted entrepreneurs can handle external judgments with grace.

10. Celebrating Progress and Growth:

Acknowledging personal growth and celebrating small achievements reinforces self-confidence. Introverted entrepreneurs can regularly celebrate their progress, no matter how incremental.

### 11. Letting Go of Perfectionism:

Perfectionism can be paralysing and contribute to the fear of public perception. Introverted entrepreneurs can let go of perfectionism and embrace imperfection as a natural part of the learning process.

### 12. Surrounding Yourself with Supportive Allies:

Introverted entrepreneurs can seek out allies who understand and appreciate their journey. These allies can provide valuable encouragement and validation during times of self-doubt.

Conclusion:

Overcoming the fear of public perception is a transformative journey for introverted entrepreneurs, empowering them to confidently own their unique entrepreneurial journey. By understanding the nature of this fear and recognizing its impact on their mindset, they can take the first step towards change. Embracing their individuality and cultivating self-confidence allows introverted entrepreneurs to shift their focus away from external judgments. Reframing negative thoughts and accepting constructive feedback enables them to navigate challenges with resilience and grace. By keeping their purpose and impact at the forefront of their actions, they stay committed to their journey despite external opinions. Embracing vulnerability and sharing their authentic selves fosters genuine connections with their audience. Building a supportive network and surrounding themselves with allies provides encouragement and reassurance. Practicing mindfulness and letting go of perfectionism liberates introverted entrepreneurs from self-imposed pressures. Celebrating progress and growth reinforces self-confidence and self-appreciation. The art of overcoming the fear of public perception transforms introverted entrepreneurs into confident and resilient trailblazers, owning their entrepreneurial journey with authenticity and purpose. By embracing their unique selves and focusing on their mission, introverted entrepreneurs leave a lasting impact on their audience and the world, proving that owning one's journey is the key to entrepreneurial success and fulfillment.

# CHAPTER 26: THE INTROVERT'S GUIDE TO NEGOTIATING: GETTING WHAT YOU DESERVE

Introduction:

Negotiating is a fundamental skill for entrepreneurs, enabling them to secure favourable deals, partnerships, and contracts. For introverted entrepreneurs, who may prefer a more reserved and contemplative approach, negotiating can be intimidating. In this chapter, we explore the art of negotiating for introverted entrepreneurs, emphasizing the significance of leveraging their introverted strengths and adopting a strategic and thoughtful approach. By mastering the art of active listening, preparing diligently, and effectively advocating for their value, introverted entrepreneurs can negotiate with confidence and get what they deserve in their business endeavours.

1. Understanding the Importance of Negotiating:

Negotiating is not just about haggling over prices; it is about advocating for one's value and interests. Introverted entrepreneurs can recognize the importance of negotiating as a means of achieving their business objectives.

2. Leveraging Introverted Strengths in Negotiations:

Introverted entrepreneurs possess inherent strengths, such as active listening, empathy, and thoughtful analysis, which are advantageous in negotiations. Leveraging these strengths empowers them to understand the other party's perspective and respond strategically.

3. Conducting Thorough Preparation:

Preparation is key to successful negotiations. Introverted entrepreneurs can diligently research and gather relevant information, enabling them to present their case confidently and knowledgeably.

4. Setting Clear Objectives:

Having clear objectives ensures that introverted entrepreneurs negotiate with purpose. By defining their desired outcomes and priorities, they can focus on achieving specific results.

5. Practicing Active Listening:

Active listening is a powerful tool in negotiations. Introverted entrepreneurs can engage in attentive listening, understanding the other party's needs and concerns to identify mutually beneficial solutions.

6. Expressing Needs and Value Effectively:

Introverted entrepreneurs may find it challenging to assert their needs and value. However, by communicating their offerings and worth effectively, they can demonstrate their expertise and contributions.

7. Managing Emotions and Nervousness:

Negotiations can evoke emotions and nervousness. Introverted entrepreneurs can manage these feelings by staying composed, taking breaks when needed, and focusing on the facts.

8. Finding Win-Win Solutions:

Win-win solutions are the goal of effective negotiations. Introverted entrepreneurs can seek creative solutions that benefit both parties, fostering long-term partnerships and collaboration.

9. Building Rapport and Trust:

Building rapport and trust are essential for successful negotiations. Introverted entrepreneurs can establish a connection by showing genuine interest and being transparent.

10. Responding to Pushback and Objections:

Pushback and objections are common in negotiations. Introverted entrepreneurs can respond calmly and confidently, addressing concerns with well-prepared arguments and evidence.

### 11. Knowing When to Walk Away:

Sometimes, walking away from a negotiation is the best decision. Introverted entrepreneurs can recognize when the terms are not favourable and have the courage to walk away if necessary.

### 12. Evaluating Negotiation Outcomes:

After negotiations, introverted entrepreneurs can evaluate the outcomes and identify areas for improvement. Learning from each negotiation experience contributes to future success.

Conclusion:

Negotiating is a transformative skill for introverted entrepreneurs, enabling them to advocate for their value and achieve their business objectives. By understanding the importance of negotiating and recognizing the strength in their introverted approach, they can confidently engage in negotiations. Thorough preparation and clear objectives provide them with a strategic advantage. Leveraging active listening and effective communication allows them to understand the other party's needs and express their value. Managing emotions and finding win-win solutions foster constructive and collaborative negotiations. Building rapport and trust establishes a strong foundation for successful outcomes. Responding to pushback and objections with confidence and evidence reinforces their credibility. Knowing when to walk away from unfavourable terms ensures they preserve their interests. Evaluating negotiation outcomes allows them to refine their approach and grow as negotiators. The art of negotiating for introverted entrepreneurs transforms them into skilled and respected advocates, securing favourable deals and partnerships. By embracing negotiation as a means of achieving their business objectives, introverted entrepreneurs make a lasting impact in their industry, confidently getting what they deserve and leaving a legacy of successful business endeavours.

# CHAPTER 27: CREATING A BALANCED WORK-LIFE INTEGRATION: FLOURISHING ON YOUR TERMS

Introduction:

Work-life balance has been a long-standing topic of concern for entrepreneurs seeking fulfillment and success in both their personal and professional lives. For introverted entrepreneurs, who may find it challenging to navigate the demands of business and personal commitments, achieving a balanced work-life integration is crucial. In this chapter, we explore the art of creating a balanced work-life integration for introverted entrepreneurs, emphasizing the significance of setting boundaries, prioritizing self-care, and aligning their work with their values. By embracing a holistic approach to life and business, introverted entrepreneurs can flourish on their terms and lead a fulfilling and sustainable entrepreneurial journey.

1. Understanding Work-Life Integration:

Work-life integration is a dynamic approach that recognizes the interconnectedness of work and personal life. Introverted entrepreneurs can understand that work and life are not mutually exclusive, but rather two parts of a whole.

2. Recognizing the Challenges of Work-Life Integration:

Introverted entrepreneurs may face unique challenges in achieving work-life integration, such as difficulty in setting boundaries and feeling overwhelmed by constant demands.

3. Setting Boundaries:

Setting boundaries is essential for work-life integration.

Introverted entrepreneurs can define specific working hours, allocate time for personal activities, and communicate their boundaries to clients and team members.

### 4. Prioritizing Self-Care:

Self-care is vital for maintaining well-being and productivity. Introverted entrepreneurs can prioritize self-care activities that align with their introverted nature, such as spending time alone to recharge.

### 5. Embracing Flexibility:

Flexibility is a key component of work-life integration. Introverted entrepreneurs can embrace flexible work arrangements that allow them to adapt to personal commitments and unexpected events.

### 6. Building a Supportive Team:

Building a supportive team enables introverted entrepreneurs to delegate tasks and responsibilities, reducing the burden of managing every aspect of their business alone.

### 7. Aligning Work with Values:

Aligning work with personal values fosters a sense of purpose and fulfillment. Introverted entrepreneurs can ensure that their business pursuits align with what truly matters to them.

### 8. Practicing Mindfulness:

Mindfulness is a powerful tool in work-life integration. By staying present and focused on the task at hand, introverted entrepreneurs can avoid distractions and maintain a healthy work-life balance.

### 9. Creating a Productive Work Environment:

A conducive work environment positively impacts productivity and work-life integration. Introverted entrepreneurs can design a workspace that promotes focus and creativity.

### 10. Integrating Personal Passions:

Integrating personal passions into their business pursuits allows introverted entrepreneurs to find joy and inspiration in their work, blurring the lines between work and personal interests.

### 11. Utilizing Technology Wisely:

Technology can be both a blessing and a curse in work-life integration. Introverted entrepreneurs can use technology wisely to enhance productivity and communication while avoiding over-dependence.

### 12. Embracing the Power of Saying No:

Saying no to commitments that do not align with their priorities allows introverted entrepreneurs to focus on what truly matters and avoid overextending themselves.

Conclusion:

Creating a balanced work-life integration is a transformative journey for introverted entrepreneurs, enabling them to flourish on their terms. By understanding work-life integration as a holistic approach and recognizing the challenges they may face, introverted entrepreneurs take the first step toward achieving balance. Setting boundaries empowers them to manage their time and energy effectively. Prioritizing self-care ensures they maintain well-being and resilience in the face of challenges. Embracing flexibility and building a supportive team allows them to adapt to the demands of both work and personal life. Aligning work with their values and integrating personal passions fosters a sense of purpose and fulfillment. Practicing mindfulness and creating a productive work environment promote focus and productivity. Utilizing technology wisely enhances their efficiency without becoming a source of stress. Embracing the power of saying no empowers introverted entrepreneurs to avoid overwhelm and focus on what truly matters. The art of creating a balanced work-life integration for introverted entrepreneurs transforms them into resilient and fulfilled individuals, leading a sustainable and meaningful entrepreneurial journey. By embracing work and life as interconnected aspects of their identity, introverted entrepreneurs create a lasting impact in their business and personal life, achieving success on their terms and leaving a legacy of harmonious work-life integration.

# CHAPTER 28: RESILIENCE IN THE FACE OF CHALLENGES: TURNING SETBACKS INTO COMEBACKS

Introduction:

Resilience is a critical trait for entrepreneurs, enabling them to navigate the inevitable challenges and setbacks that arise in the entrepreneurial journey. For introverted entrepreneurs, who may be more introspective and sensitive to external pressures, developing resilience is especially vital. In this chapter, we explore the art of cultivating resilience for introverted entrepreneurs, emphasizing the significance of adopting a growth mindset, learning from failures, and leveraging their introverted strengths to bounce back stronger from adversity. By embracing challenges as opportunities for growth and remaining steadfast in their pursuit of success, introverted entrepreneurs can turn setbacks into powerful comebacks and forge a path to lasting achievement.

1. Understanding Resilience:

Resilience is the ability to bounce back from adversity, setbacks, and failure. Introverted entrepreneurs can understand that resilience is not about avoiding challenges but about embracing them as stepping stones to success.

2. Recognizing the Challenges of Resilience:

Introverted entrepreneurs may face specific challenges in developing resilience, such as coping with self-doubt and overcoming their sensitivity to criticism.

3. Cultivating a Growth Mindset:

A growth mindset is fundamental to resilience. Introverted entrepreneurs can embrace challenges as opportunities for learning and improvement, rather than viewing them as insurmountable obstacles.

4.  Learning from Failures and Setbacks:

Failures and setbacks are inevitable in entrepreneurship. Introverted entrepreneurs can learn from these experiences, extracting valuable lessons to inform their future decisions and actions.

5.  Developing Emotional Intelligence:

Emotional intelligence is crucial in building resilience. Introverted entrepreneurs can develop emotional awareness and regulation, allowing them to navigate challenges with composure and perspective.

6.  Seeking Support from a Supportive Network:

A supportive network is a valuable resource for building resilience. Introverted entrepreneurs can lean on friends, family, mentors, and like-minded individuals for encouragement and advice.

7.  Practicing Self-Compassion:

Practicing self-compassion enables introverted entrepreneurs to treat themselves with kindness and understanding during challenging times, fostering resilience and self-belief.

8.  Embracing Solitude for Reflection:

Introverted entrepreneurs can use their natural inclination for solitude as a tool for reflection and introspection, gaining clarity and perspective during difficult situations.

9.  Setting Realistic Expectations:

Setting realistic expectations for themselves and their businesses helps introverted entrepreneurs avoid unnecessary pressure and disappointment.

10. Finding Strength in Vulnerability:

Vulnerability is a source of strength, not weakness. Introverted entrepreneurs can embrace vulnerability as a means of connecting with others and seeking support during tough times.

### 11. Maintaining a Long-Term Perspective:

Maintaining a long-term perspective allows introverted entrepreneurs to see setbacks as temporary challenges on their path to success.

### 12. Celebrating Resilience Milestones:

Celebrating milestones of resilience reinforces positive reinforcement and motivation. Introverted entrepreneurs can acknowledge their progress and growth as they overcome challenges.

Conclusion:

Cultivating resilience in the face of challenges is a transformative journey for introverted entrepreneurs, enabling them to turn setbacks into powerful comebacks. By understanding resilience as the ability to bounce back and grow from adversity, they set the foundation for success. Recognizing the challenges of resilience empowers introverted entrepreneurs to confront and overcome their unique obstacles. Cultivating a growth mindset reframes challenges as opportunities for learning and improvement. Learning from failures and setbacks transforms introverted entrepreneurs into adaptive and knowledgeable leaders. Developing emotional intelligence equips them with the tools to navigate challenges with composure and perspective. Seeking support from a supportive network provides encouragement and guidance during difficult times. Practicing self-compassion fosters resilience and self-belief. Embracing solitude for reflection allows introverted entrepreneurs to gain clarity and wisdom. Setting realistic expectations avoids unnecessary pressure and stress. Finding strength in vulnerability fosters authentic connections and support. Maintaining a long-term perspective provides a sense of direction during challenging moments. Celebrating resilience milestones reinforces motivation and positive reinforcement. The art of cultivating resilience for introverted entrepreneurs transforms them into strong and resilient leaders, capable of overcoming any obstacle on their path to success. By embracing challenges as opportunities for growth and maintaining unwavering determination, introverted entrepreneurs make a lasting impact in their business and in the lives of others, proving that resilience is the key to turning setbacks into comebacks and achieving enduring success in their entrepreneurial journey.

# CHAPTER 29: FOSTERING GROWTH MINDSET: EMBRACING LEARNING AND ADAPTABILITY

Introduction:

A growth mindset is a powerful mindset that fuels personal and professional development. For introverted entrepreneurs, who may face self-doubt and resistance to change, cultivating a growth mindset is essential for overcoming challenges and achieving continuous growth. In this chapter, we explore the art of fostering a growth mindset for introverted entrepreneurs, emphasizing the significance of embracing a love for learning, embracing adaptability, and reframing setbacks as opportunities for improvement. By cultivating a growth mindset, introverted entrepreneurs can unlock their full potential, embrace change, and thrive in their entrepreneurial journey.

1. Understanding the Power of a Growth Mindset:

A growth mindset is the belief that abilities and intelligence can be developed through dedication and hard work. Introverted entrepreneurs can understand the transformative power of this mindset in their personal and professional growth.

2. Recognizing the Challenges of Cultivating a Growth Mindset:

Cultivating a growth mindset may be challenging for introverted entrepreneurs who are naturally cautious and may fear stepping out of their comfort zones.

3. Embracing a Love for Learning:

A love for learning is at the core of a growth mindset. Introverted entrepreneurs can cultivate curiosity and seek opportunities for continuous learning and skill enhancement.

4.  Viewing Challenges as Opportunities:

Introverted entrepreneurs can reframe challenges and setbacks as opportunities for growth and improvement, recognizing that mistakes and failures are part of the learning process.

5.  Embracing Adaptability:

Adaptability is a crucial skill for introverted entrepreneurs to navigate the ever-changing business landscape. Embracing adaptability allows them to stay agile and responsive to market trends.

6.  Taking Calculated Risks:

A growth mindset encourages introverted entrepreneurs to take calculated risks, recognizing that stepping outside their comfort zones can lead to new opportunities and growth.

7.  Seeking Feedback for Growth:

Seeking feedback is an essential aspect of a growth mindset. Introverted entrepreneurs can actively solicit feedback from mentors, customers, and team members to identify areas for improvement.

8.  Setting Stretch Goals:

Setting stretch goals challenges introverted entrepreneurs to go beyond their perceived limitations, encouraging them to aim higher and achieve more significant milestones.

9.  Developing Resilience in the Face of Setbacks:

Resilience is integral to a growth mindset. Introverted entrepreneurs can develop resilience by bouncing back from setbacks and using them as stepping stones to success.

10. Celebrating Progress and Effort:

Introverted entrepreneurs can celebrate their progress and efforts along the way, reinforcing the value of hard work and dedication in their journey of growth.

11. Practicing Positive Self-Talk:

Positive self-talk is a powerful tool in fostering a growth mindset. Introverted entrepreneurs can cultivate self-encouragement and affirmations to boost their self-belief.

### 12. Creating a Growth-Focused Environment:

Building a growth-focused environment within their business encourages introverted entrepreneurs and their team members to embrace continuous learning and improvement.

Conclusion:

Fostering a growth mindset is a transformative journey for introverted entrepreneurs, enabling them to embrace learning, adaptability, and continuous improvement. By understanding the power of a growth mindset, they set the foundation for personal and professional growth. Recognizing the challenges of cultivating a growth mindset empowers introverted entrepreneurs to overcome their natural resistance to change. Embracing a love for learning fuels curiosity and drives them to seek continuous improvement. Viewing challenges as opportunities reframes setbacks as stepping stones to success. Embracing adaptability allows them to thrive in an ever-changing business landscape. Taking calculated risks expands their horizons and opens new opportunities. Seeking feedback fosters a culture of growth and learning within their business. Setting stretch goals challenges them to reach new heights of achievement. Developing resilience equips them to bounce back from setbacks and remain steadfast in their pursuit of growth. Celebrating progress and effort reinforces the value of dedication and hard work. Practicing positive self-talk empowers introverted entrepreneurs with self-belief and confidence. Creating a growth-focused environment encourages learning and improvement among team members. The art of fostering a growth mindset for introverted entrepreneurs transforms them into resilient and adaptive leaders, capable of embracing change and thriving in their entrepreneurial journey. By cultivating a growth mindset, introverted entrepreneurs make a lasting impact in their business and in the lives of their team members, proving that embracing learning, adaptability, and continuous improvement is the key to unlocking their full potential and achieving extraordinary success in their entrepreneurial journey.

# CHAPTER 30: CELEBRATING INTROVERTED ENTREPRENEURSHIP: YOUR JOURNEY TO SUCCESS

Introduction:

Celebrating introverted entrepreneurship is about acknowledging and embracing the unique qualities and strengths that introverted individuals bring to the world of business. For too long, introverts may have felt overshadowed or underestimated in the entrepreneurial landscape, but the truth is that their introverted nature can be a powerful asset in building successful ventures. In this chapter, we explore the art of celebrating introverted entrepreneurship, emphasizing the significance of authenticity, creativity, and the power of quiet leadership. By recognizing and amplifying their unique strengths, introverted entrepreneurs can carve a path to success that aligns with their true selves and leaves a lasting impact on their industry and the world.

1. Understanding the Power of Introverted Entrepreneurship:

Introverted entrepreneurship is not a limitation but a unique approach to business. Introverts can understand the value they bring to the table and appreciate the different perspective they offer.

2. Embracing Authenticity:

Authenticity is the cornerstone of introverted entrepreneurship. By embracing their true selves and staying true to their values, introverted entrepreneurs can build businesses with integrity and purpose.

3.  Recognizing the Strength of Introverted Leadership:

Introverted leaders possess qualities such as active listening, empathy, and thoughtfulness that can inspire and motivate their teams. Recognizing the strength of introverted leadership empowers entrepreneurs to lead with grace and impact.

4.  Cultivating Creative Problem-Solving:

Introverted entrepreneurs often excel in creative problem-solving. By tapping into their imaginative minds and introspective nature, they can devise innovative solutions to complex challenges.

5.  Leveraging the Power of Solitude:

Solitude is a source of creativity and clarity for introverted entrepreneurs. They can leverage quiet moments to brainstorm ideas, plan strategies, and make insightful decisions.

6.  Nurturing Introverted Networking:

Introverted networking may differ from traditional networking, but it is equally valuable. By focusing on building deep and meaningful connections, introverted entrepreneurs can create a strong support system.

7.  Utilizing Intuition in Decision-Making:

Introverted entrepreneurs possess a strong sense of intuition. By trusting their gut instincts and combining them with data-driven analysis, they can make well-informed decisions.

8.  Embracing Thoughtful Communication:

Thoughtful communication is a hallmark of introverted entrepreneurship. By choosing their words carefully and delivering messages with intention, they foster meaningful connections with clients and stakeholders.

9. Transforming Vulnerability into Strength:

Vulnerability is not a weakness; it is a strength. Introverted entrepreneurs can recognize the power of vulnerability in building trust and authenticity in their relationships.

### 10. Creating a Quiet Space for Innovation:

Introverted entrepreneurs can create quiet spaces within their businesses to promote innovation and creativity. These spaces allow team members to think deeply and generate novel ideas.

### 11. Balancing Productivity and Rest:

Balancing productivity with adequate rest is crucial for introverted entrepreneurs' well-being. By honouring their need for solitude and downtime, they can maintain long-term productivity and creativity.

### 12. Leaving a Legacy of Impact:

Introverted entrepreneurship is about leaving a legacy of impact that goes beyond financial success. By focusing on meaningful contributions and positive change, introverted entrepreneurs make a lasting difference.

Conclusion:

Celebrating introverted entrepreneurship is a transformative journey for entrepreneurs who embrace their introverted nature as a source of strength and innovation. Understanding the power of introverted entrepreneurship allows them to step confidently into the entrepreneurial landscape. Embracing authenticity fosters businesses built on integrity and purpose. Recognizing the strength of introverted leadership enables them to lead with grace and impact. Cultivating creative problem-solving fuels innovation and competitive advantage. Leveraging the power of solitude allows for deep introspection and insightful decision-making. Nurturing introverted networking builds a strong support system. Utilizing intuition in decision-making combines instinct and data-driven analysis. Embracing thoughtful communication fosters genuine connections with stakeholders. Transforming vulnerability into strength builds trust and authenticity. Creating quiet spaces for innovation promotes creativity within their businesses. Balancing productivity and rest ensure long-term well-being and success. Leaving a legacy of impact goes beyond financial achievements and contributes to positive change. The art of celebrating introverted entrepreneurship transforms introverted entrepreneurs into trailblazers, making a significant impact in their industry and leaving a legacy of authenticity and purpose. By embracing their unique strengths and staying true to their authentic selves, introverted entrepreneurs inspire others to do the same and create a business landscape that celebrates diversity and innovation. As they celebrate introverted entrepreneurship, they prove that quiet leadership and introspective minds are essential for shaping a successful and meaningful entrepreneurial journey.

# EPILOGUE

As we come to the end of "Personal Development for Introverted Entrepreneurs," we hope that this journey has been transformative, empowering, and enlightening for you. Throughout these pages, we have explored the unique strengths and qualities that introverted entrepreneurs possess, and we have celebrated the power of quiet leadership, deep thought, and authentic connections.

In this epilogue, we want to remind you that your introverted nature is not a hindrance, but a gift that sets you apart in the entrepreneurial world. Embrace your introverted self, for it is your wellspring of creativity, empathy, and resilience. Embrace your ability to listen actively, to reflect deeply, and to make thoughtful decisions. Embrace the strength in vulnerability, as it builds trust and authenticity in your relationships.

As you venture forth in your entrepreneurial journey, remember that personal growth is a continuous process. Embrace each setback as an opportunity to learn and grow. Allow yourself to adapt to change, for it is in the midst of change that innovation and creativity thrive.

Stay true to your values and principles, for they will guide you through the challenges that come your way. Nurture your passion and curiosity, as they will fuel your desire for continuous learning and improvement. Celebrate your progress and efforts, no matter how small they may seem, for they are stepping stones to greater achievements.

Know that the road to success is not linear, and it is okay to take detours, explore new paths, and revisit your goals. Along the way, you will encounter both triumphs and failures, but it is in these moments that your resilience will shine through.

Surround yourself with a supportive network of like-minded individuals who understand and appreciate your introverted approach. Seek mentors who can guide and inspire you on your journey, and be open to offering support to others who may be walking a similar path.

As you embrace your introverted entrepreneurial journey, remember that there is no one-size-fits-all formula for success. The beauty of entrepreneurship lies in its diversity, and the impact you make will be unique to you. Celebrate your wins and learn from your losses, for each experience shapes you into the remarkable entrepreneur you are destined to become.

In the vast landscape of entrepreneurship, introverted entrepreneurs bring a rare and valuable perspective. As you embrace your introverted nature, you will find your voice amidst the noise, and your quiet leadership will inspire those around you. This book is not an end but a beginning—a beginning of a new chapter in your life as an introverted entrepreneur. May it serve as a source of inspiration and guidance whenever you need it.

In closing, we celebrate you—your authenticity, your resilience, and your unwavering determination. Embrace your introverted entrepreneurial journey with confidence and pride, for you possess the power to create a lasting impact in the world.

Congratulations on your journey to success as an introverted entrepreneur. The world awaits the unique contributions only you can bring.

With warm regards,
Shah Rukh